Sunita Rajwade

The Fragrance of Mango Blossoms

Exploring the culinary traditions of the Kokanastha Brahmin

Popular Prakashan
www.popularprakashan.com

Published by
POPULAR PRAKASHAN PVT. LTD.
301, Mahalaxmi Chambers
22, Bhulabhai Desai Road
Mumbai – 400 026
www.popularprakashan.com

First Published 2014
First Reprint November 2014

(4326)
ISBN: 978-81-7991-767-1

Design: Anjali Sawant
Typesetting: Chetna Singh

Printed in India
by Repro India Ltd.
Navi Mumbai - 400 710

Dedication and Acknowledgments

This book of gastronomic memories is dedicated to my family, who never fails to appreciate the food I put before them; my friends, well-wishers, and all those who made sure that I actually got my act together and wrote down the words that make up this book.

This book would have not been possible were it not for the unstinted support given to me by my mother, mother-in-law, several aunts and uncles. Thank you, especially Sheila *kaki* and Vedika, who have been generous with their inputs of shared food memories and folklore.

Foreword

My earliest memory is of the pressure cooker hissing away as my grandmother got the lunch ready. This terrifying hiss would be accompanied with an unforgettable aroma which spread all over the house and lingered on long after the hissing stopped. The distinct fragrance of Ambemohar rice (Mango Blossom rice) is typical in Maharashtrian households who love their rice soft and sticky. This small grained rice is rounded and brittle and grows along the foot hills of Western Maharashtra.

With globalisation being the new *mantra*, there is an increased awareness about Indian food. This is largely due to the emergence of a new breed of Indian restaurants that has broken free of the traditional stereotype of sleaze and grease claiming to be 'Taj Mahals' and 'Bombay Palaces' serving high quality food. Several eateries serving less well-known regional cuisines such as *idli* and *dosa*, Goan *balchao*, Bohri curry, Hyderabadi *biryani* and wonder of wonders even some vegetarian fare, have now made Indian food chic and trendy.

But, despite transcending the threshold of *tandoori* chicken, *samosa* and curry-rice, the food eaten by my community remains a mystery to most of my compatriots, as it does to the rest of the world. This is not surprising really because we are known to be a people who value our space, closely guard our privacy and very rarely serve our traditional cuisine to outsiders.

Another reason for our cuisine remaining unfamiliar to most is the fact that our everyday home cooking has changed thanks to urbanisation, the breakdown of traditional joint families, and with globalisation blurring cultural identities. Spices from the North and South have transformed our traditional way of cooking, and have changed forever the *dal* and rice our grannies used to cook.

In addition, our own forays into the big, wide world have introduced our palates to myriad tantalising tastes, rendering our typical food boring and bland by comparison. We have abandoned our traditions and completely identified with the 'modern' world. Regrettably, we are more comfortable with pizzas and pastas than *puri* and *bhaaji*. Thus, while many of us may not know much about *Chaturthi* and *Ekadashi*, we will happily tell you when Mother's Day will be this year! But, there are still a few of us around who sometimes remember things from the past — the slowly vanishing tastes of our childhood and festivals celebrated in the traditional way.

Sadly, not only are these fading memories, but they face the threat of vanishing completely as there are now fewer and fewer people who remember the past, a fact brought home to me when I actually started writing out traditional recipes for my own daughters to follow. Not only were certain foods unfamiliar to them, but they had no idea of how and why certain festivals are celebrated.

I realised that there were several things that I myself didn't know, and began to look to an older generation to help me out. And I soon found that most of our grandmothers have either passed away, or are unable to remember, and our mothers have often been too involved in living in modern times to recollect what it was like when they were growing up! It occurred to me that the source of recipes and folklore was slowly depleting, and that there was a need to record a tradition that had hitherto been passed down from generation to generation just by word of mouth. Thus a search for recipes changed into a journey seeking to record the customs and traditions of my community.

As I said earlier, this is not a compendium of all the *Kokanastha* customs, rituals and recipes. The information that I have gathered regarding the customs and rituals is from friends and relatives. I have made some comments about our community but not with the intention of offending any one and apologise for hurting any sentiments albeit inadvertently. Please treat this book as an affectionate commentary on the customs and food of our community.

Happy eating and happy reading!

— Sunita Rajwade
2014

Contents

Introduction

At the risk of sounding chauvinistic, *Kokanastha* food is considered nothing short of perfect. At least this was the personal view of one of my husband's many aunts. I can never forget how she would preen like a queen as she sat at the head of the table, watching with pride and satisfaction, the food being wolfed down by her friends and family, declaring with smug pride, "And do you know our simple *Brahmini* food is the best and most healthy? And it is also the most complete meal!" She would then go on to substantiate her claim by citing the authority of the World Health Organisation (with strong emphasis on every word), which she claims certified our food as such. How she came by this information I still cannot fathom, as I cannot imagine any WHO official sitting through one of our almost never-ending meals, burping his satisfaction (as is the customary show of appreciation), and then working out the calorific and nutritional values in a laboratory.

But there is perhaps some truth to her statement, because if eaten the way it was meant to be — a simple menu of *bhaat*, *bhaaji* and *poli*, eaten day in and day out — it is undoubtedly a meal that perfectly addresses our bodies' dietary requirement of protein, carbohydrates, fat, sugar, fibre and vitamins, while pandering to all the five tastes: sweet, sour, savoury or salty, bitter and pungent. Most recipes serve four, but you can alter the proportions according to the number of people you plan to serve.

FOOD AND RITUALS

Food and rituals are deeply intertwined in our everyday life. For instance, a person embarking on a journey will invariably be offered three helpings of *dahi* or sugar by the lady of the house to ensure a safe return.

Similarly, in a simple ceremony called *drishta kadhne* the evil eye is warded off from a person (normally a young child) who may suddenly be drawing attention to himself either by his good health, good looks or just general good luck. The ceremony is performed ideally at sunset by the child's mother, grandmother, or the oldest woman in the house, who tightly clenches black mustard seeds and salt in both fists and waves her arms in a circular motion over the person three times drawing out all the negative vibes. She then touches the feet of the person, cracks her knuckles and flings the contents of her fist into the crackling fire.

In our normal everyday worship we offer our gods a thanksgiving (*nevidya*) of a simple fruit or sugar or a small bowl (*vati*) of milk and sugar, much like the one that my grandmother used to offer to her gods, and which I would greedily drink up at the end of the day! In our own little *devghar* or altar, I often come across an offering of *gool khobra* (jaggery and coconut) which I later discover to be my mother-in-law's token of gratitude for the help she has received from God whenever she has had any misgivings or misapprehensions.

The humble *supari* or betel nut is absolutely essential for worship, and is even used in a routine *owalni*, a ritual in which the blessings of the Almighty on the honoree are sought by the person doing the *ovalni*. This ritual is generally performed to welcome someone to the home, or during festivals like *Padva*, *Bhaubeej*, or on a special day like a birthday. During the *ovalni* the person sits or stands in an east-west direction. His forehead is marked with vermilion, a few grains of rice sprinkled on his head and saffron water dabbed on his forearms. A betel nut is circled over his head and a tray bearing a lighted oil lamp is moved in a circle before him, bathing him in a warm glow of light.

Certain foods like *sheera* are absolutely essential for an important religious ceremony like the *Satyanarayan Pooja*, as is the *panchamrut* or five sacred foods - milk, sugar, honey, yoghurt and ghee (*toop*). Similarly, popped wheat or *lhaaya* is always associated with *hom* and *havan* (purification by fire), where the fire is stoked with offerings of *toop* and *lhaaya*.

A ritual mainly associated with rural *Kokanasthas* is the *Muhurtha Mel* a ritual where five married women, each of whom has both her parents and parents-in-law alive, are invited to grind the wheat in the house of the bride-to-be. The idea being to ensure that the new bride also enjoys the good fortune of having both her parents and parents-in-law to enrich her own life. The flour that is ground is made into dough and fashioned into *ghavlya*, *maltya* and *nakhulya* which can be best understood as types of pasta. This ceremony is accompanied by folk songs and hymns, invoking blessings for the young bride.

Ghavlya which look like tiny grains of wheat are fashioned by rolling the dough between the thumb and forefinger, the rolling signifying the tough times that the bride may have to withstand. *Maltya* which are fashioned by rolling out the dough on the stone *sahan* (flat stone for making sandalwood paste) are twirly bits signifying the twists and turns the bride may face on life's journey.

Similarly, *nakhulya* which are made by nicking bits of dough with a nail, signify the barbs and taunts the bride may face in her new home. The idea behind this ceremony is to ward off any of these hardships a bride may encounter, and to enable her to brace herself and face them with fortitude should the occasion arise. The *ghavlya*, *maltya* and *nakhulya* are then sun-dried and made into a *kheer* (sweet porridge) which is offered to the son-in-law, to further ensure that the bride goes to her new home with the blessings and protection of her maternal home.

The remainder of this dough is stored in a box with some *halad-kunku* (turmeric and vermilion) in the middle of the *devghar*, or in the store room representing Ganpati or Lord Ganesh, the protector, who keeps misfortune at bay. After the wedding ceremony, the Ganpati is immersed in a river or pond. Like most of our rituals, this ceremony too has been modified, as the delayed age of marriage amongst today's brides means there are very few women who have both sets of parents alive to bless the new bride. This ceremony is conducted on any day around a week prior to the wedding, except on *amavasya* (new-moon days).

During the *barse* or naming ceremony, sprouted red *chana* is placed below the cradle. These sprouted beans which have germinated signify life, and when placed under the cradle signify the hope that yet another life will come along soon!

HOME AND HEARTH

The kitchen is the heart of the home, and of equal importance is the store room or *talghar*, which gets its name from the original position of the storehouse which was in the basement of the house. Naturally basements are defunct these days in Indian homes, and so is the custom of storing food grains for the entire year.

But there are still some homes that observe the tradition of an annual stocking up of rice, wheat and *dal* (pulses) in huge storage drums with *neem* leaves scattered inside to prevent the weevils from attacking the produce.

Large families even today have stockpiles of pickles, preserves, *papad* and spices, sharing space with the staples of rice, wheat and other cereals. This space was naturally out of bounds for most, and visits to the store room were strictly monitored.

Families owning large tracts of farmland would generally reserve their own produce for consumption, while others would stock their pantries with store-bought produce. Large brass storage drums that were polished to perfection, or empty sixteen-kilogram biscuit or *vanaspati* tins were used to store grain. Those were the times when it was difficult to shop every day, and a single visitor or whole families would drop by without any notice.

CUSTOMS AND CULTURE

Apart from a few special customs like the *bondla* (a special ritual for girls during *Dassera*) and *bodan* (a ritual performed by a married woman), *Kokanastha Brahmin* follow the traditions of all *Maharashrian Brahmin*. A feature that distinguishes our customs is the use of *puran* to make *divas* (lamps) for the *ovalni*. Unlike most people who make these lamps with plain wheat flour dough, we prefer to make them out of the same sweetened gram flour which is used to make our famed *puran poli*.

In traditional households, fathers literally brought home the 'bacon', stopping on their way home from work to pick up fresh vegetables for the evening meal. I still remember how my uncle used to stop at the local market on his way home from his high-powered job. Gradually of course this chore was taken over by the women folk, but this strong gene in *Kokanastha* men is automatically activated when it comes to shopping for groceries. Unwilling to do any other housework, this is one task they most love performing — wandering through the lanes and choosing between this vegetable and that. It is no wonder then that in most homes, menu choices are dependent on the likes and dislikes of the man of the house.

As in most Hindu homes, menstruating women were barred from the kitchen, and at 'that time of the month' actually ate separately from the rest of the family. Purity was of such importance that the kitchen was actually out of bounds for everyone apart from the cook. And the cook could only enter the kitchen after a bath, and dressing herself in freshly laundered clothes. No one was supposed to talk or even touch the cook (*sohala*), and if by chance the cook was defiled by however slight a physical contact with a person, she had to bathe all over again. But of course, neither of these customs is followed these days.

VEGETARIANISM AND THE KOKANASTHA BRAHMIN

Despite our patriarchal society, it is well-known that the hand that rocks the cradle actually rules the world. And *Kokanastha* women are no different from the rest. While we get our names from our fathers, we get our sense of self from our mothers, more specifically, the food that they feed us. For a community that prides itself on being above crass materialism, frowning upon the pursuit of pleasure and wealth, we give undue importance to something as material and basic as food. We are obsessed with what goes into our stomachs and what comes out! All my life I have heard the litany – "have this – it is good for you" "you are what you eat", "this will make you big and strong!" and other such persuasive homilies. While this is a generic trait of every mother, irrespective of her cultural background, I would like to think that we *Kokanastha* women have made this into a science and a way of life. Not only is food eaten for its nutritive value but also for its medicinal value. It is no wonder then that longevity is a dominant gene in our community: we live long and we live healthy. Each family has stories of uncles and aunts or grandfathers and grandmothers who lived well into their full Biblical quota of four score and ten years, with all their teeth and wits intact, and who could bravely fight off real or make-believe intruders, and do vigorous battle over some imagined slight, their frailness or age notwithstanding.

Apart from our genes, our good health can be attributed to the fact that we are pure vegetarians. Freshness and seasonality of food are of prime importance, and vegetables and fruit are eaten strictly according to season.

Ruchira, the revered Marathi recipe book is considered to be the most complete documentation of *Kokanastha* food. Authored by Kamalabai Ogale and first published in March 1970, it is the bible of several Maharashtrian housewives of my generation, myself included. Usha Jategaonkar has also translated parts of it into English. People of my mother's generation often used it as a reference book especially to put to rest a point of dispute.

The Fragrance of Mango Blossoms focuses on two major aspects, the first dealing with our daily bread and the second dealing with our folklore, rituals and the foods associated with them. I hope you enjoy this culinary journey as much as I have enjoyed rediscovering it myself!

Wholesome Food

Like the upfront *Kokanastha* people, our food is a utilitarian and wholesome no-nonsense vegetarian fare. It is nourishing and spiced ever so delicately, with just a dash of sugar to round off any rough edges. Rice is the staple grain and is eaten in every form and at almost every meal as a main course or a side dish, as a dessert or a savoury snack.

SERVING FOOD

A plated meal is the best way to serve this cuisine. The advantage of a plated meal is that all the food is served at once and all of it is eaten, because wasting food is definitely forbidden! While the traditional banana leaf has given way to more contemporary tableware, the rules of serving food remain the same.

Starting with salt at the top of the plate, going clockwise you have a *vati* of *aamti*, a *vati* of *rassa* (or some other gravied dish) followed by a serving of bhaaji with puri or *poli* served in the centre. On the other side of the plate is placed a wedge of lime, some chutney, pickle and *koshimbir*.

The order in which these are placed is very important, because if salt is served after the pickle, there is a chance of the oil getting into it. Similarly, it is important to serve salt first because the only time salt is not served is when the food is offered as *nevidya* to the gods, or served during funeral rites.

Everyday meals are served in the more practical *taat* a large platter familiar to most as a *thali*. With a diameter of 12-14 inches and a slightly raised edge, *taat* are generally made of stainless steel, brass, silver and occasionally, even gold! Yes, I have heard stories of some erstwhile royal families who used to have stacks of golden *taat* which were used exclusively by members of the family for special occasions like weddings, unmindful of the fact that the rest of the guests ate off the pedestrian banana leaf. But the *taat* too, like the banana leaf, has vanished from several homes, as they are cumbersome and difficult to clean and store.

However, the banana leaf has not completely vanished from our lives and the practice of eating off the leaf is still observed at community meals like weddings, *munja* (thread ceremonies) and *pooja*, or at special sit-down meals at home where the disposable banana leaf is the best way of eliminating washing dishes!

According to tradition, all the leaves are lined up longitudinally, in front of a row of wooden *paat* (low wooden seats) for the people to sit on. To the left of the *taat*, close to the *paat*, is placed the individual *tambya* (copper glass) or simple *bhanda* for water. Generally, people are called to eat only after all the plates are filled with a small serving of each dish.

At large functions, people are served in batches, sittings or *pangat*; and even today, on an everyday basis, particularly in large joint families, the men of the house and the children are served at the first sitting by the ladies of the house, who hover around attending to their every whim. While this may sound chauvinistic, it actually makes sense for the women to get things out of the way and then settle down to eat later, undisturbed and in peace. In fact, I remember my grandmother telling me that a wife had to eat what was left in her husband's plate and you could tell by the amount of food he left in his plate how well he thought of his wife! For instance, if he was annoyed with her, she could very well find herself eating just a few morsels while on a day he was very happy, she could also eat her fill, so it was in her interest to keep her husband happy! I don't really know how far this custom is true, but I do remember that when I protested at this demeaning and insulting way of treating women, my grandmother defended it as an eco-friendly custom where two people could eat out of one leaf, thereby saving on leaves! Thankfully the leaf was not washed and re-used for another meal, but actually fed to the family cow.

Sitting at the *pangat* can spark off many family feuds because very often people are called to the table in order of their status, the honoured guests eating in the first round and the family or hosts eating in the last one. Once the food is served, everyone is invited to eat and after all are seated, a short prayer or grace before meals marks the signal to begin eating. It is customary to sprinkle a little water around the *taat* or banana leaf before eating. This, apparently was an effective barrier to inquisitive ants or other creepy crawlies that might otherwise walk into your plate! During the course of the meal, second and third helpings are offered making sure that every guest eats to his or her heart's content. It is no wonder then, that every guest is advised to "eat slowly, to savour every morsel and to extend that meal into one long, sensory experience".

TABLE MANNERS

It is considered extremely rude to ask the guest if he has had enough, and the server is supposed to keep serving till told to stop! This ensures that the person who is being served actually concentrates on what is happening. A guest who is too busy talking to his neighbour, may find the rice piling up to his chin, because rice is not served with a spoon, but shovelled onto the plate or leaf.

Since the *pangat* is a community meal it is considered boorish and disrespectful to walk away from the *pangat* after finishing one's meal. When the last person has finished eating, the crumbs around the leaf are neatly picked up and placed on the leaf which is folded up. Leaving a banana leaf unfolded or walking away from the *pangat* by stepping over the leaf will set many heads shaking and many tongues wagging, bemoaning the lack of good manners and breeding. So it is only after every person in the *pangat* has finished eating can one get up and leave.

It is my belief that good food is enjoyed best when eaten with one's fingers. But while eating, care should be taken that the food is eaten delicately without slopping it around, making sure that no food gets on to one's palm. As children we were discouraged from playing with food or doodling in the plate, and found it strange that you could slurp your *aamti* and *kadhi* but not lick your fingers. I still remember drawing designs in the *taat* only to have my uncle reprimand me, saying that it was bad luck and if I did so, my mother would die! Obviously this was a ridiculous statement, but it did serve to remind me for the rest of my life that I couldn't ever play with the food in my plate.

THE BASICS AND PANCHAPAKWAAN

After the first serving of rice, fresh *poli* are served. Seconds are offered freely and the meal is rounded off with yoghurt and rice or *dahi bhaat*. This is a normal, basic, everyday meal which would be an ideal meal, when people did real work and burned up real calories. I am sure if one were to eat like this every day, it would mean more than an extra hour on the treadmill! Today, as with most things, this meal has been modified and a regular meal consists of either rice or *poli* being served at each meal, along with just one *bhaaji* and either *rassa* or *aamti*.

So essentially, Kokanastha food is all about BBP or *Bhaat*, *Bhaaji* and *Poli*. *Bhaat* in its most basic form is just plain steamed rice. *Bhaaji* is the vegetable that is generally confined to the specialty of the season. *Poli* is specifically a *Kokanastha* word for the unleavened flatbread known as *chapati* to the rest of the world. The best *poli* is a thin, flaky flatbread like a *paratha*, slightly crisp and browned on the outside and tantalisingly tempting with the fragrance of *toop* (clarified butter).

This basic diet is modified daily with add-ons like *koshimbir*, chutney, pickles, *papad* according to the season and occasion. On special days, the food is more elaborate with the *poli* being substituted by fat, fried *puri*, an additional *bhaaji*, an additional side dish and perhaps a sweet like *shrikhand* or *kheer*. *Kokanasthas* are known for their extra-sweet tooth, and sweets are an integral part of the meal with a bite of the sweet interspersed with the savoury. Special meals are called *panchapakwaan* or a meal with five special sweets. There would also be richly flavoured *masale bhaat* in addition to the two normal rice courses! Of course, a typical meal was often rounded off with a good *paan* and I remember how fascinated I was with the autocratic way in which Indu *maushi* used to call for her silver *paanacha daba*, which she would ceremoniously open, chop the *supari* into tiny bits, add a little bit of *kaath* to the *paan*, add some *gulkand*, fold it into a triangle, push a clove in to hold it all together and then hand it to us with a flourish.

THE ESSENTIAL KITCHEN

While there is nothing like a typical *Kokanastha* kitchen, there are some of us with faint recollections of our grandmothers' kitchens: bare, functional and dark. Often, they had cold, clammy stone floors or in rare cases dung-plastered floors, with the strong smell of wet earth (much like the smell of fresh rain) emanating from the *maath* or clay water pot. I used to love to dip the long handled ladle into the pot to fill up my glass, or open the small tap at the bottom of my other granny's *maath*, or better still, when she was particularly indulgent, actually stir the alum around in the water to make it safe to drink. The rows of gleaming copper and brass pots neatly lined up on open shelves, a bunch of onions hanging on the wall, a small piece of wire strung up with dusty dog-eared electricity bills, the sharp smell of lemons sharing the tiny space on the window sill blending with the crisp fragrance of coriander stored in a water-filled jam jar; and the slow rising vapour from the pot of boiling water, made my granny's kitchen seem mysterious and magical. The constant admonitions to keep away from the kerosene stove, to be mindful of the live coals, to ensure that the wire mesh shutters of the cupboards were properly shut, to be careful that I did not spill or drop anything, only made me feel that the kitchen was a very special place to which only the truly deserving were allowed entry.

And the tiny cupboard with wire mesh shutters fitted into a niche in the wall, also known as *dubhatyacha kapaat* in which she stored milk or left the *dahi* to set, would also be used to keep small change on hand for any tradesman who came to the door. What a contrast this is to our well-planned kitchens of today, equipped with state of the art refrigerators, microwave ovens, electric mixers and dishwashers!

POTS AND PANS

Strange as it may sound, five pots are all that is required in a *Kokanastha* kitchen, frugality being part of our genetic make up. Of course this is in addition to all the other stuff that is required to cook including the stove but essentially, five pots are integral to every bride's trousseau much like the five *sarees* that she brings with her into her marital home.

With the extra effort required to maintain brass and copper pots, traditional cookware is fast becoming obsolete and can either be found in antique shops or dusty attics, waiting patiently to be dragged into a modern home to be used as planters or decorative pieces. The fact that the *kalaiwala* (tinsmiths) too are a dying breed does nothing to stem this trend. I would like to mention that a pot is a pot is a pot, but at the same time the shape of the pot can affect the outcome. So it is important to cook in the right pot: after all something like a *puri* cannot be deep-fried on a *tawa*!

Kadai: This wok-like vessel needs no introduction as most kitchens have a similar looking pot. The traditional *kadai* is made of iron (the thicker and heavier the better) with two riveted handles for easy handling. Some housewives swear that the *kadai* should never be scrubbed clean, only rinsed out so that the accumulating rust increases the iron intake in one's food. A heavy gauge iron *kadai* makes sense as it prevents the food from sticking and makes for even frying.

Ganza: A tall narrow pot useful for boiling milk or anything that boils and bubbles over. I often use it to churn buttermilk and love watching the cream collect at the top.

Tapela: The *tapela* with its narrow brim and wide bottom is used for boiling water.

Paatela: The *paatela* which comes in various diameters is used for making rice and dal.

Langdi: Wide-based shallow *langdi* are used to make vegetables, like stuffed aubergines, that need to be spread out while cooking.

Tawa: A cast iron griddle used to cook *poli* and other flatbreads.

Polpaat Laatna: The rolling pin (*laatna*) and board (*polpaat*) are essential to make *poli* and *puri*.

Vili: The coconut grater or *vili* is unfortunately dying out since it can only be used effectively while squatting on the floor. The *vili* is anchored by putting one's foot on the wooden base with the blade opened out. The round jagged end of the blade is used as a grater while the sharp curved blade is used to slice and cut vegetables, an operation that requires intense concentration and care, because one false move could have disastrous consequences! Funnily enough, people who have used this contraption vouch for it completely and swear that the sharpest knife cannot match its efficacy.

Paata Varvanta: This traditional stone *masala* grinder has to be kept in good shape by a traditional *takiwalli* who scores the ridges in the stone with a chisel. However, with more convenient ways to grind *masala* pastes this kitchen accessory is becoming obsolete. The *varvanta*, the round stone that is actually used to pulverise the chutney comes into its own during the *barse* or naming ceremony of the child. At the beginning of the ceremony, the *varvanta* is disguised as the infant in the traditional *kunchi* (cape), and passed over and below the cradle by the grannies in an effort to confuse any evil spirits that might be hovering around.

Ravi: A wooden churner for blending *dal* and making buttermilk.

Chimta: Metal tongs are essential to keep the pot in place while its contents are being vigorously stirred.

Jata: Another totally obsolete gadget, but one which was constantly on my husband's 80-year-old aunt's bed is the *jata*. This contraption is the original domestic grinding mill consisting of two stone discs one on top of the other with the upper one turned around by a short stubby handle. Even though Indu *tai* was too old to do any housework, she used to diligently grind a handful of wheat each day, an activity that made her break out into a sweat. Unable to hold back my curiosity as to why she performed this seemingly useless task, she told me that this was the best form of exercise which we modern day housewives seem to have forgotten! Considering that her own mother lived to almost a hundred, and the fact that she herself soon crossed this milestone, there may be some truth to this.

Pimpa: This brass or copper pot to store water comes into its own during the wedding of a daughter. Traditionally the girl's family places the printed invitation inside this vessel and presents it to the groom's family to invite them to the wedding. This strange bit of information came to me during my own daughter's wedding, when one sister-in-law asked me if I had invited the in-laws. I thought it strange to invite them to their own son's wedding, and even stranger to deliver the invitation inside a water pot, but since this is what she herself had done, I assumed it to be a custom that has long since gone out of favour, and is prevalent only among the truly orthodox *Kokanasthas*.

Also useful is the assortment of stirrers and spoons like the *zhara* or slotted spoon for draining the oil while frying *puri* or making *boondi*, and the *ulatna* to flip over *poli* and *ghavan*.

Now with the cooking implements in place, all that is needed are the actual ingredients. Our food is basically vegetarian and since we believe there are very few vegetables with an innate flavour, most vegetables need a bit of spice to make them appealing to the palate. So adding the right kind of spice and the right amount of spice is very important, and what is more important, is having those spices always at hand. Before going into the actual recipes, I would like to mention that I have used the word cup as a measure because it is most convenient. This is equal to a 200 ml cup. Some ingredients are measured in cups or teaspoons while at other times this is given in actual weight. This inconsistency is largely due to the fact that sometimes these small quantities cannot accurately be measured. In any case, as my father always tells me, as long as the food tastes good, you shouldn't really be nitpicking about the tiniest gram. So with a little bit of adjustment here and there, you will find that the food on your table is much appreciated.

Masale, Toop ani Phodni

SPICE MIXES, GHEE AND SEASONING

THE SPICE BOX OR MISALNYACHA DABBA

In an old-fashioned kitchen, this would be a flat round brass box with tiny containers that neatly fit within to hold the *masala* for about a week. This convenient method of storage ensured that there was no mad rush for the turmeric while the mustard seeds burned - a common mistake when making the *phodni* or seasoning. As with most utensils, stainless steel has replaced the brass dabba. The spices commonly used are *halad* (turmeric powder), *tikhat* (red chilli powder), *garam masala* (ground spice mix), *mohri* (whole mustard seeds), *jeera* (cumin seeds), and powdered *hing* (asafoetida). Of course the contents of the *dabba* depend on one's own personal preferences.

Not to be found in a *masala dabba* is saffron, which plays an important role in a *Kokanastha* kitchen and during rituals. This very expensive spice, normally kept under lock and key, is used on all special occasions and adds a distinct flavour and aroma to sweets like *kheer*, *shira*, *shrikhand*, *laadoo*, *karanji* and *modak*. It is no wonder then that this spice is made into a delicate paste and applied to the forearms of a person who is being specially honoured during the *ovalni* on a special occasion like the pre-wedding family dinner (*kelvan*), or on a special birthday. This wonderfully fragrant paste truly makes one feel special and festive.

While ready-made *masala* are a boon for today's busy housewife, a true cook will know the difference between home-made spice powders and ready-made concoctions. Unlike our strong grannies, who had to pound their *masala* in the *khal-batta* or mortar and pestle, we can without any effort at all pulverise our secret ingredients in an electric mill or coffee grinder. These home-ground powders can be stored in airtight containers in the cool confines of a refrigerator or freezer to retain their freshness for several months.

Goda Masala - I

TRADITIONAL SPICE MIX - I

Its name translates as 'sweet spice mix' but there is nothing sweet about this spice blend which is unique to Maharashtrian cooking. A ground blend of coriander seeds, red chillies and dried coconut among other ingredients, it is traditionally made by pounding the ingredients in a *khal-batta*. *Goda Masala* is common to all Maharashtrian food but what makes *Kokanastha goda masala* different from the others is its deep, dark colour which comes from unpolished black sesame seeds. The proportion of the ingredients used for this *masala* varies from family to family but this is the recipe I have been following, which was given to me by my mother.

Ingredients

2-3 tablespoons oil
250 grams coriander seeds
60 grams cumin seeds
1 tablespoon black peppercorns
60 grams whole dried red chillies
6-7 cinnamon sticks
30 grams cloves
½ dried coconut, grated
60 grams black unpolished sesame seeds
3-4 tablespoons rock salt

Method

- Heat the oil in a *kadai* and roast the coriander and cumin seeds, stirring all the time to ensure they are uniformly roasted. When the aroma of the roasted spices is released, take the *kadai* off the heat, remove the spices and set aside.
- In the same *kadai*, roast the peppercorns, red chillies, cinnamon sticks and cloves. Once again, set aside.
- Lastly, roast the grated coconut and sesame seeds.
- Cool the ingredients and grind into a fine powder. Add some rock or common salt and store in an airtight jar. This *masala* generally lasts me for around 3 months or so, but will vary according to its usage.

Makes 300 grams

Note: Dried coconut is available as a *vati* or half a dried coconut. Use the dark unpolished sesame seeds to impart a black colour to the mix. If you want this *masala* to last for more than 6 months at room temperature you should avoid using the coconut. Refrigerate if using coconut.

Goda Masala – II

TRADITIONAL SPICE MIX - II

This is possibly a more traditional recipe.

Ingredients

½ cup sesame seeds
2-3 tablespoons oil
10 grams asafoetida (*hing*)
160 grams coriander seeds
½ dried coconut, grated
¼ cup cumin seeds
3 teaspoons caraway seeds (*shahi jeera*)
2 heaped teaspoons cloves
4-5 (3-inch long) cinnamon sticks
5-6 bay leaves
2-3 star anise (*chakri phool*)
1 heaped teaspoon turmeric powder
½ cup red chilli powder
¼ cup salt

Method

- Dry-roast the sesame seeds in a *kadai* and set aside.
- Add the oil to the *kadai* and roast the asafoetida.
- Then roast the rest of the spices and mix all the roasted spices together.
- Allow to cool and then grind to make the *masala*.

Makes 300 grams

Note: You could add 1 teaspoon fenugreek seeds or mustard seeds if desired. *Goda Masala* is particularly used in Aamti (page 51), Masaale Bhaat (page 40), stuffed vegetables like Bharli Vaangi (page 80) and Bharli Karli (page 81).

Kandyacha Masala

TRADITIONAL SPICE MIX WITH ONIONS

A delicious variation of the regular *goda masala* is the onion or *kaanda* added to the *goda masala*.

Ingredients

½ kg onions
3 tablespoons oil
½ dried coconut, cut into pieces
2 large whole garlic bulbs
1 recipe Goda Masala (page 24, 25)
1 cup red chilli powder
1 cup fresh coriander

Method

- Slice the onions finely and dry them in the sun.
- Then roast in hot oil the onions, coconut and garlic.
- Grind and add to the already ground *goda masala*.
- Lastly add the chilli powder and coriander and fry in the remaining oil.
- Mix well with all the ground spices to get *kandyacha masala*.

Note: The other popular *masala* mixes are Garam Masala (page 27) and Kachacha Masala (page 28).

Garam Masala

ROASTED SPICE MIX

Ingredients

½ teaspoon oil
20-30 cloves
20-30 black peppercorns
1 teaspoon fenugreek seeds
40 grams coriander seeds
2 x 3-inch cinnamon sticks
4 teaspoons cumin seeds
4 teaspoons black cumin seeds (*shah jeera*)
12 black cardamoms
2 teaspoons mustard seeds
12 bay leaves
5 star anise (*chakri phool*)
2 teaspoons cobra saffron (*nagkesar*)

Method

- Heat the oil in a pan. Add the cloves, peppercorns and fenugreek seeds and roast well stirring all the time. Take off the heat.
- Roast the remaining ingredients.
- Grind them all together.
- Store in an airtight jar.

Note: I must admit that I do not normally use this *masala* and when I checked with my mother, she says that she has never used fenugreek seeds, but this is a variation of her own spice mix.

Kachcha Masala

SUN-DRIED SPICE MIX

This speciality *masala* that is used for Rassa (page 61), Masaale Bhaat (page 40) and Khichadi (page 36) is different from the rest of the *masala* because the spices are not roasted, but toasted in the sun. Needless to say this *masala* cannot be made during the monsoons or wet months, because what really makes it flavourful is the brilliant sunshine it soaks up. If it is stored for a long time, it loses its zing so it should be made in small quantities and used up almost immediately.

Ingredients

20 grams coriander seeds
4 tablespoons cumin seeds
2 teaspoons black cumin (*shah jeera*)
10-12 cloves
3-inch cinnamon stick
1½ teaspoons asafoetida (*hing*)

Method

As mentioned earlier, these should be sun-dried for a while before grinding.

Makes 300 grams

COMMONLY USED INGREDIENTS:

Other ingredients that are handy to have around are:

Coconut: Being essentially a coastal people, it is only natural that we generously use coconut in our cuisine – both as a curry base and as a garnish. Sometimes the milk extracted from the coconut is used as an alternative to water for cooking. Fresh coconut milk can easily be substituted by tinned coconut milk or even dried coconut milk powder that can be reconstituted with water.

Kokum: *Garcinia Indica* is the botanical name for this fruit which is commonly used as a souring agent in many coastal cuisines of India. It is generally found in our homes as dried rinds.

Gool: The first stage in sugar manufacture yields a golden brown mass of unrefined sugar known as jaggery or *gool*. Travelling through the countryside during winter or after the cane harvest, the smoke curling up from the *gurhal* or clay oven is a common sight. It is rich in iron and has a strong rustic taste.

Oil: The oil we normally use is groundnut oil which is referred to as *goda tel* in all Marathi cookbooks. I myself find that any other cooking oil can be substituted (except of course sesame oil and mustard oil) without really compromising on the taste.

Toop: Since *toop* is the secret ingredient that transforms the ordinary to the divine, it is important to make the right kind of *toop*, and deserves its own recipe.

Saadi Phodni

BASIC SEASONING

The base of all our vegetables and *dal* is a simple seasoning of oil and mustard seeds known in Marathi as *phodni*.

Ingredients

1-2 teaspoons oil (depending on one's preference and also the quantity of vegetable to be cooked)

¼-½ teaspoon mustard seeds

A pinch of asafoetida (*hing*)

½ -1 teaspoon turmeric powder

Method

- Heat the oil in a pan.
- Add mustard seeds and when they start to splutter, add the asafoetida and turmeric powder and immediately remove from heat or add the rest of the ingredients.

Note: *Bhaaji* that require this simple seasoning are cabbage, French beans, sliced potato, ladies' fingers, cauliflower, and all leafy greens. This seasoning is also used to make *usal* and *dal*. A variation of this seasoning calls for ghee (*toop*) to substitute oil, cumin powder instead of the mustard seeds and a pinch of asafoetida with some curry leaves. This seasoning is used for Masaale Khichadi (page 37), Kadhi (page 60) and for *bhaaji* that require to be cooked in coconut milk.

Toop

CLARIFIED BUTTER

Ingredients

Cream collected from whole milk
for at least a fortnight

1 teaspoon yoghurt

Method

- Boil the milk and skim off the cream which settles on top after the milk has cooled. Refrigrate the cream.
- After about 2 days collection, add the yoghurt or *dahi* to the cream and stir well. It is advisable to stir the mixture every day to prevent the cream from turning rancid or smelling. The collected cream should also be kept refrigerated.
- After about two weeks, when enough cream has been collected, keep the pot out the whole night so that the cream sets into a firm yoghurt.
- Churn the set yoghurt/cream with a *ravi* or an electric beater. Cover with cold water and leave to rest. The water helps bind the butter together and also washes off any faint smell. (Actually, it should not have any smell, for, if it does smell, then it is an indication that it is rancid).
- Drain off the buttermilk or *taak* which can be used to make Kadhi (page 60) or Suralichya Vadya (page 212).
- Transfer the solid white butter to a heavy-bottomed pan and cook on a high heat, stirring continuously, to prevent it from burning, and also to release the trapped air that makes the whole mixture rise to the top of the pan. Lower the heat when the mixture begins to separate into a golden yellow liquid (*toop*) and a brownish/white solid that sinks to the bottom (*beri*).
- When the liquid begins to bubble, sprinkle a little water and when you hear a crackling sound, the *toop* is done. Allow the *toop* to cool a while and then drain off the liquid part and throw away the brown *beri*.
- When it cools you will get a whitish, granular viscous jelly like substance called *toop*.

Note: A true *Kokanastha* would use up the *beri* while kneading the flour for *polis*, but to be honest, I have never ever come across anyone who has done this. I have even heard of some people sprinkling powdered sugar over the *beri* to make a yummy sweet and once again I confess, I myself have never tried it. However, the divine distillate enhances the flavour of the humblest of dishes like *chapati* and of course when poured generously over *puran poli* or *varan bhaat* they are immediately transformed into manna from heaven. I must warn you that *toop* making is quite a tedious and messy affair: expect your hands to get greasy and sticky and be prepared for a strong smell to permeate your home and hair.

Now that you have the right kitchen with all the right ingredients, you should be well equipped to take on the task of bringing to your table wholesome food.

So, now what differentiates *Kokanastha* cuisine from other Maharashtrian food? Actually, what really differentiates one kitchen from the next is the grandmother otherwise known as...

THE AJJI

The secret weapon in *Kokanastha* households is *ajji*, the most important person in the family and the kitchen. She is the grandmother who is the true mover and shaker of not only the cradle but the entire world. Therefore, I feel that 'Le must de *Kokanastha* cuisine' is an *ajji*, or presiding grandmother. The genuine article would be a fat little lady, rather like an unsteady Pooh Bear with her scanty hair barely covering her balding pate, pulled back into a tiny little knot of a bun, her nine-yard *saree* displaying a generous amount of leg and her ample bosom covered with a snuggly wrapped *pallu*, one end tucked firmly at the waist.

The *ajji* is essential not only to cook food the right way, but also to maintain the family tradition and honour. A real *ajji*, would begin the day early with a bath, a freshly washed *saree* and head straight to her personal domain. The traditional system known as *sohala* which forbade any one from entering the kitchen and polluting it by their presence, was actually the perfect way of ensuring complete concentration and getting things done in peaceful solitude.

In addition to the *ajji*, or in lieu of her, *kakus* and *maamis* along with *maushis* and *atyas* and of course the ever present *aiee* would also qualify to be the keepers of the faith and guardians of the family's secret recipes. Daily menus are simple with dietary rules to be followed. We eat vegetables according to the season, grains according to the weather and even festival menus are predetermined. Before we go any further I must mention that the recipes in this book are meant to serve 4 people eating a regular meal of *dal* (lentils), *bhaat* (rice), *bhaaji* (vegetables) and *poli* (flatbread).

Everyday Food

Our every day food is so simple that some might even label it tasteless and bland, since it is neither floating in oil, nor so over-spiced as to leave you gasping for water. Sometimes when I look at the various snacks available at Health Food shops, I am reminded of my granny's home-made snacks: tasty and almost fat-free. There is a skill in producing meals that are delicious without the aid of strong spices and oil. Apart from the basic rice and/or *poli*, seasonal vegetables, sprouted beans and a well-made *dal* is what is eaten every day.

Home-made pickles, fresh chutney and some fried food on the side, add variety to the meal which is normally rounded off with *dahi* or *taak*. It may surprise many but traditional *Kokanastha* food does not even use onions and garlic. As my father-in-law never fails to remind me, while he was growing up, he had never seen an onion in his home. Even today, his brother has banned garlic from his table!

Having been totally brainwashed into believing what you eat is what you become, I now understand why we are the way we are. All of us have been nurtured on a wholesome diet of *varan bhaat*. This very simple dish, which normally consists of mushy overcooked rice, squished lovingly by the *ajji* together with bland yellow dal; generously doused with pure ghee (*toop*) and a squeeze of lime can make the most seasoned gourmet drool.

Even someone with little or no interest in food cannot fail to get emotional at the thought or mention of *varan bhaat*, for this was our first introduction to food. I doubt there exists a *Kokanastha Brahmin* who has not been weaned on this favourite nursery food. So important is the dish that even at the grandest of grand feasts, a truly satiated *Brahmin* can only belch his satisfaction after that last bit of *varan bhaat* slides down his throat.

Bhaat

RICE DISHES

To begin at the beginning, our nursery food like all nursery food is bland, nutritious and tasty. *Varan bhaat* is the first adult food our palates are introduced to, and its distinct taste remains embedded in our memories forever, and as is the case with comfort foods, the first thing we reach out to in troubled times.

Like all classics, this dish is made with very simple ingredients – *ḍal* and *bhaat*. Traditionally, the amount of rice required for one meal is estimated by a simple formula: a fistful of rice for each person with an extra fistful thrown in for the additional person who might wander in at mealtime. So if the rice at the table falls short, you could always blame the cook and her small hands!

It is obvious that perfect *varan bhaat* needs the perfect ingredients. This may be a personal preference, but to my mind, the best *varan bhaat* can only be made from a good quality Ambemohar or what I love to translate as Mango Blossom rice. This stubby, short and wonderfully aromatic grain is so named, because of the delicate fragrance of delicate Mango blossoms that perfumes the air while it is cooking.

Sadly this rice has given way to more hardy varieties and the modern day *Indrayani* rice is the closest alternative available these days. *Indrayani* is a specially developed hybrid strain that retains the delicate flavour of Ambemohar while being a hardier crop.

As the rice gurgles in the pot, the rich, tempting, irresistible aroma of Ambemohar announces to all and sundry that dinner is about to be served and quickly brings everyone to the table. This burn-your-tongue hot food is a passion with most *Kokanastha Brahmin* who literally like their food so freshly made, that it goes straight from the fire into the mouth!

Another food fetish is the practice of eating only freshly made food, which is so ingrained into our subconscious making most of us still cringe at seeing a refrigerator stuffed with leftovers. I for one while using the convenience of a freezer, still find it hard to eat food that has been frozen for a year.

Varan

BASIC SPLIT PIGEON PEA CURRY

This *dal* made from the humble yellow legume known as split pigeon peas or *tuvar dal* and is the perfect accompaniment to sticky Ambemohar.

Ingredients

1 cup split pigeon peas
¼ teaspoon turmeric powder
A pinch of asafoetida (*hing*)
1 teaspoon salt
A pinch of sugar
A dollop of ghee (*toop*)
Lime slices

Method

- Wash and soak the lentils for 10 minutes.
- Drain and add 2½ cups of water, turmeric, asafoetida and salt.
- Place the lentils in a pressure-cooker and cook till the pressure is released 2-3 times (2-3 whistles).
- Gently mash the *dal* into a purée with the traditional *ravi* or with a wire whisk.

Note: Add a pinch of sugar and serve hot over hot rice with a generous dollop of ghee (*toop*) and a wedge of lime.

Bhaat

STEAMED RICE

Ingredients

1 cup Ambemohar
or any short-grained rice

1½ cups water
A pinch of salt

Method

- Wash the rice and drain. Repeat the process, until the water runs clear.
- Soak the rice for at least 10 minutes so that it softens and cooks faster.
- Drain and transfer to a heavy-bottomed pan with 1½ cups of water and a pinch of salt.
- Place the pan on high heat and when the water begins to boil, lower the heat and cook, covered, till all the water is absorbed and the rice is soft.
- Turn off the heat, and leave the pan covered for 2 minutes.
- Serve hot with Varan (page 34).

Note: It is important to cook the rice in just the right amount of water to ensure that all the nutrients are retained because we don't believe in pouring off the excess water. *Varan bhaat* can easily be made in one go by cooking the rice and the *dal* separately but in one pressure cooker. In this case, 1 cup rice should be cooked in 1½ cups of water, while 1 cup of *dal* is cooked in 2½ cups of water. The *dal* should be placed below the rice, and covered well, to prevent it from boiling over while being cooked. The container should be placed on a trivet with about ½ cup of water. Cook for 5 minutes or till the pressure is released 3 times (3 whistles). Allow the pressure to reduce by itself, as this gives the food inside that much more time to cook.

Once your *varan* and *bhaat* are ready, all you need is a loving *ajji* to squish them together into a homogenous mass, jazz it up with a generous blob of ghee (*toop*) and a squeeze of lime and feed you bite by bite, while every other cousin waits his turn open-mouthed, as she tells you the endless story of the crow and the sparrow. *Sadha varan poli*, another nursery delight, is a mishmash of Varan (page 34) and Poli (page 130) doused in warm molten ghee (*toop*).

Khichadi

SOFT RICE WITH GREEN GRAM

Having eaten this mushy yellow concoction for almost every day of my childhood, I vowed never to serve this dish at my own table. However, as they say, the apple never falls far from the tree, and when my own babies came along, I naturally gravitated to this familiar baby food. For me, the soft and squishy *pich-pich khichadi*, drowning in *toop* with its seductive smell lulling you to a peaceful slumber, is synonymous with baby talcum, cuddles and giggles. I am convinced that this deceptively simple dish is the real health food that makes for strong teeth and healthy bones largely because of its wholesome nutritive value. At any rate, this dish is also given to convalescents and people who want to rebuild their strength, because it is easy on the digestive system and power-packed with nutrients to fight attacking germs!

Apart from babies, this dish offers a lot of comfort to upset stomachs or tired souls. Eaten with crisply fried *papad*, you can crunch away your feeling of sadness and be transported back to those baby days when nothing went wrong.

Ingredients

⅔ cup rice
⅓ cup split green gram (*moong dal*)
A pinch of asafoetida (*hing*)
2 teaspoons ghee (*toop*)
¼ teaspoon turmeric powder
Salt to taste
½ teaspoon cumin seeds (optional) (see note)

Method

- Wash and soak the rice and split gram together for 10 minutes.
- In a pressure cooker, add the rice and split gram, asafoetida, ghee, turmeric powder and salt and cook till the pressure is released twice (2 whistles).
- Alternatively, to cook *khichadi* in a pan, add all the ingredients and cook on high heat. When the mixture starts to boil, lower the heat, and cook until soft.
- Serve hot with fried *papad*.

Note: Alternatively, you could fry cumin seeds and asafoetida in a little ghee (*toop*), add the rice and *moong dal* together and sauté for a few minutes.

Masaale Khichadi

SPICY RICE WITH GREEN GRAM

This is a *khichadi* for more mature palates and is especially welcome on rainy days.

Ingredients

1 cup rice
½ cup split green gram (*moong dal*)
1 teaspoon oil
¼ teaspoon mustard seeds
¼ teaspoon cumin seeds
¼ teaspoon turmeric powder
A pinch of asafoetida (*hing*)
2-3 curry leaves
1 onion, finely sliced (optional)
1-2 cloves
½ teaspoon red chilli powder
1½ teaspoons Goda Masala (page 24, 25) (optional)
Salt to taste

Method

- Wash and soak the rice and split green gram for 10 minutes.
- Heat the oil in a pan; add the mustard seeds and when they start to splutter, add cumin seeds, turmeric powder, asafoetida, and curry leaves.
- Add the onion and sauté till pink.
- Add the rice and *dal* and continue frying.
- Add the cloves, chilli powder and *goda masala* and fry a little longer.
- Add 2 or 3 cups of water and salt to taste and cook until soft. The amount of water you add to the rice will depend on how soft and mushy you would like the *khichadi* to be.

Methkoot Bhaat

SPICED RICE GRUEL

Rice is our favourite food and nothing can be yummier than the simple rice gruel (Maou Bhaat (page 39)) eaten with a delicately spiced powder called *methkoot*. This finely blended mix spices up several dishes which need to be just slightly spiced and in fact a very close relationship between two individuals is often described as *methkoot*, signifying the complete harmony between all the ingredients. *Methkoot bhaat* is a simpler alternative to *khichadi*.

Ingredients

1 cup split Bengal gram
2 cups split black gram (*urad dal*)
½ cup rice
¼ cup wheat
¼ cup mustard seeds
2 teaspoons cumin seeds
2 teaspoons coriander seeds
2-3 dried red chillies
1-inch dried turmeric
2 teaspoons asafoetida (*hing*)
1-inch dried ginger
½ nutmeg

Method

- On a *tawa*, separately dry-roast all the ingredients, except asafoetida, ginger and nutmeg, until light brown and fragrant. Cool.
- Grind together all the roasted spices, asafoetida, ginger and nutmeg to a fine powder.
- Store in an airtight container.
- Add *methkoot* and *toop* to taste, to hot Maou Bhaat (page 39) and serve.

Note: This blend of powdered *dal* and spices is just the right teaser for a jaded appetite, or a rebellious stomach.

Maou Bhaat

RICE GRUEL

The rice served with *methkoot* is aptly described as gruel, and to make the perfect gruel you would need the perfect rice – Ambemohar. Alternatively, an equally aromatic rice like the *Basmati* would do just as well.

Ingredients

1 teaspoon + 2 teaspoons ghee (*toop*), to serve
2-3 peppercorns
1 teaspoon finely chopped ginger
1 cup Bhaat (page 35)
Salt to taste

Method

- Heat the ghee in a pan. Add the peppercorns, ginger, and cooked rice.
- Add salt and as much water as required and mash the rice till it acquires a porridge-like consistency.
- Add ghee and serve hot with *methkoot*.

Note: It isn't always necessary to make *methkoot bhaat* out of rice gruel, plain steamed rice will also do. I also know of some people who like to flavour their *dahi* with *methkoot*!

FOOD FOR US MERE MORTALS

A perfect balance of food groups and low in fat, our everyday food is easy to prepare and easy to digest. Apart from the rice and *poli*, which are staples, you must have *bhaaji* (vegetables), *usal* (gravied legumes), and *koshimbir* (salads) and some yoghurt at the end of the meal.

The low-lying and narrow Konkan strip is ideal for the cultivation of rice, coconuts, mango and cashew nuts; which is why rice and coconuts are absolutely integral to our meal. Rice is cooked in several ways and is eaten both as a savoury dish and as a sweet. It is eaten every day in the form of the humble Varan Bhaat (page 34, 35), or the cooling Dahi Bhaat (page 46). Jazzed up with exotic spices and vegetables, it is cherished as *masaale bhaat* on very special occasions like weddings and *pooja* celebrations. Surprisingly, *Kokanasthas* who are otherwise known to be tight-fisted are very generous with their servings of rice. Guests are treated with courtesy and hospitality and it is a matter of pride that they are personally served by the ladies of the house. With their *padar*, the loose end of the *saree* thrown over the shoulder, tucked in at the waist and out of the way, the ladies of the house, bent over at the waist and with straight knees, shovel the rice on to the guest's *taat* till he signals his satisfaction.

But thanks to recent diet fads, rice is increasingly becoming a no-no. Not only is *varan bhaat* becoming a delicacy relegated to nursery days, but even *masaale bhaat* which was once obligatory at weddings, is fast vanishing, and being replaced by the more universally appealing vegetable *pulao*. This is a shame really as old timers can swear that the obligatory burp signifying deep satisfaction comes easier after mounds of lip-smacking flavourful *masaale bhaat* generously drizzled with piping hot *toop*. I remember at one time, the subtlety of the *masaale bhaat*, particularly at weddings, was discussed with as much interest as the behaviour of outcast relatives. So for those of you who value authenticity, *masaale bhaat* is actually the hallmark of a *Kokanastha* feast and you would do well to master its secrets. In fact a good *masaale bhaat* can give any *biryani* a run for its money!

Masaale Bhaat

SPICED RICE WITH IVY GOURD

Ingredients

1 cup short grained rice
2 cups long slices of ivy gourd (*tondli*)
2 teaspoons Goda Masala (page 24, 25)
10 cashew nuts, soaked
2 teaspoons salt
A pinch of sugar or jaggery
½ cup thick yoghurt, beaten
2 teaspoons chopped coriander
½ cup freshly grated coconut

Spice paste

1 teaspoon cumin seeds
1 teaspoon coriander powder
1 whole dried red chilli
1-inch piece dried coconut

Seasoning

2 tablespoons oil
1 teaspoon mustard seeds
2-3 curry leaves
A pinch of asafoetida (*hing*)

Method

- Wash and drain the rice and set aside for at least half an hour.
- For the spice paste, dry-roast the cumin seeds, coriander powder, and red chilli on a *tawa*. Grind together with dried coconut, to make a fine paste.
- For the seasoning, heat oil in a heavy-bottomed pan, and add the mustard seeds. When they start to splutter, add curry leaves and asafoetida.
- Add the rice and sliced ivy gourd and sauté on medium heat for 5 minutes.
- In the meanwhile, bring 2 cups of water to a boil; add to the rice, and cook, covered, till the rice is almost tender.
- Add the spice paste, *goda masala*, cashew nuts, salt and sugar. Stir and cook, covered, on low heat for 5 minutes.
- Stir in the yoghurt, cover and cook for 5 minutes longer.
- Just before serving, garnish with chopped coriander and freshly grated coconut.

Note: While traditionally this dish is made with ivy gourd, it can be substituted with brinjals to make another classic, *vaangi bhaat*. For *vaangi bhaat*, soak small quartered brinjals, as required, in water to prevent browning and remove the slight bitter aftertaste some brinjals have. Brinjals take a long while to cook so they should be sautéed before the rice is added. Alternatively, if you hate both these vegetables, you could use peas, cauliflower, cabbage, green capsicums, ridge gourd, green tomatoes and even sprouted field beans (recipe follows).

Dalimbyacha Masaale Bhaat

SPICED RICE WITH SPROUTED BEANS

These tiny brown, slightly bitter, field beans (*dalimbi/val*) are a favourite of *Kokanasthas*, and some preparation of this bean is *de rigeur* on a really special occasion.

Ingredients

1 cup rice

1 cup sprouted and peeled field beans (see note)

1 teaspoon Goda Masala (page 24, 25)

2 teaspoons coriander powder

1 teaspoon cumin powder

½ teaspoon red chilli powder

Salt to taste

A pinch of sugar

2 tablespoons chopped coriander

1 fried dried red chilli

2 tablespoons freshly grated coconut

Seasoning

2 tablespoons oil

½ teaspoon mustard seeds

½ teaspoon turmeric powder

A pinch of asafoetida (*hing*)

2-3 curry leaves

Method

- Wash and drain the rice and set aside for 30 minutes.
- For the seasoning, heat the oil in a pan; add the mustard seeds and when they start to splutter, add turmeric, asafoetida and curry leaves.
- Add the rice and sauté for 2-3 minutes.
- Then add the sprouts and continue frying.
- In the meanwhile, boil water and add to the rice.
- Cook, covered, on low heat, for 5 minutes.
- When the rice is half cooked, add *goda masala*, coriander, cumin and chilli powders, salt and a pinch of sugar. Cook, covered, until the rice is tender.
- Serve hot, garnished with chopped coriander, fried chilli, and grated coconut.

Note: Soak the dried beans overnight. Drain and leave to sprout for 24 hours in a sprouter, or tie in a piece of muslin or cotton cloth and leave to sprout in a dark corner of the kitchen. Peel off the skin. Immersing the sprouted beans in warm water for around 5 minutes helps loosen the skin which is then easier to remove.

As mentioned earlier, this *masaale bhaat* is truly an acquired taste because bitter beans are not very popular. However, true connoisseurs of *Kokanastha* food love the bitter taste that comes with the soft beans that crumble in the mouth. It is a shame that not only has this dish lost its popularity, but the bitter bean itself is an endangered species, commonly substituted with its country cousin goda *vaal*, but nothing can replicate the joy of tucking into a bowl of *dalimbyacha bhaat*.

Ravan Bhaat

SPICED RICE COOKED IN BUTTERMILK

Ingredients

2 tablespoons oil
1 teaspoon turmeric powder
¼ teaspoon asafoetida (*hing*)
2-3 curry leaves
2 cups rice
4 cups buttermilk
1 cup split Bengal gram, soaked
1 cup roasted and powdered sesame seeds
½ teaspoon powdered dried fenugreek seeds
2-3 pieces tamarind, soaked and pulp extracted

Seasoning

2 teaspoons oil
2-3 dried red chillies

Method

- Heat oil in a pan and add turmeric, asafoetida and curry leaves.
- Add the rice and sauté for 2-3 minutes.
- Add the buttermilk and cook until the rice is done.
- Transfer the rice to a bowl and mix together the soaked gram, powdered sesame seeds, powdered fenugreek seeds, and tamarind extract.
- For the seasoning, heat oil in a pan; add the dried chillies and mix into the rice.
- Serve hot.

Golyacha Bhaat

SPICED RICE WITH DUMPLINGS

Ingredients

2 cups rice
4 tablespoons oil + for shallow frying (optional)
1 teaspoon salt
A pinch of sugar
A dash of lime juice
1 teaspoon chopped fresh coriander
2 tablespoons freshly grated coconut

Dumplings

2 tablespoons oil
½ teaspoon turmeric powder
A pinch of asafoetida (*hing*)
1 cup coarsely ground gram flour (*besan*)
1 teaspoon coriander powder
½ teaspoon cumin powder
½ teaspoon red chilli powder
¼ cup roasted groundnut powder
2 tablespoons desiccated coconut
Salt to taste

Method

- To make the dumplings, heat the oil in a pan; add turmeric and asafoetida and sauté for a few seconds.
- Add the gram flour and sauté for a few minutes till fragrant. Remove from the heat.
- Add coriander, cumin and chilli powders, groundnut powder, desiccated coconut and salt. Knead together to make a dough, cover and set aside for half an hour.
- Divide the dough into small marble-sized balls. Fry the dumplings in a little oil until light brown. Remove and set aside. Alternatively, steam the dumplings in a colandar or steamer till done.
- For the rice, wash and drain the rice and set aside for half an hour.
- Heat the oil in a pan; add the rice and sauté for a few minutes. Simultaneously, bring 1½ cups of water to a boil and add to the rice, along with the salt, sugar and a dash of lime juice. Cook, covered, for 5 minutes.
- When the rice is almost done, place the fried dumplings on top, cover the pan and leave to gently steam for another 5 minutes.
- When the rice is tender, check if the dumplings are cooked, and gently stir them into the rice so they do not break up.

- Serve with individually drizzling fresh tempering made without turmeric on each helping. Serve hot, garnished with chopped coriander and grated coconut.

Tamate Bhaat

TOMATO RICE

My dad used to love this squishy rice and my mother makes it for almost every family occasion. I love its sweet and sour taste with a strong aroma of cinnamon.

Ingredients

1 cup rice
2 tablespoons ghee (*toop*)
1 teaspoon sliced ginger
2 slit green chillies
2 bay leaves
2 cloves
¼ teaspoon powdered cinnamon
1 onion, finely chopped
4-5 soaked cashew nuts
1 cup tomato purée
¾ cup coconut milk
Salt to taste
1 tablespoon chopped coriander

Method

- Wash and drain the rice, and set aside.
- Heat the ghee in a pan and add ginger, green chillies, bay leaves, cloves and cinnamon powder.
- Add the onion, and fry until pink.
- Add rice and fry for another 2 minutes.
- Add the cashew nuts and tomato purée and cook for 5 minutes.
- Add the coconut milk and salt and bring to a gentle boil. Lower the heat, cover the pan and simmer till the rice is tender.
- Serve hot, sprinkled with chopped coriander.

Butti Bhaat/Dahi Bhaat

YOGHURT RICE

Nothing is more welcome than *butti bhaat* after a long, hot and tiring day. With a dash of spicy mango pickle and the accompanying crunch of fried *papad*, it becomes even more heavenly. At one time, long overnight train journeys also meant *butti bhaat*, its cool comfort providing the perfect foil to a dusty, overcrowded compartment. Simple it may be, but it is fickle indeed and a slight rise in temperature can render it sour and unpalatabe.

Ingredients

1 cup cooked Bhaat (page 35)
½ cup yoghurt
½ cup milk
A pinch of salt
Sugar to taste

Seasoning

2 tablespoons ghee (*toop*)
1 teaspoon cumin seeds
2-3 curry leaves
1 dried red chilli or stuffed red chilli (*bharleli mirchi*)

Method

- For the seasoning, heat the ghee in a pan, and add cumin seeds, curry leaves, and chilli and take off the heat.
- Mash the rice and add the yoghurt, milk, the seasoning and a pinch of salt and sugar to round it off.
- Serve hot, with mango pickle or fried *pohyache papad*.

Note: If *butti bhaat* is to be eaten 4 hours or so later, reduce the yoghurt to 2 tablespoons and add some more milk which will turn into yoghurt during the course of the day, and prevent the rice from turning sour.

Saakhar Bhaat

SWEETENED RICE

As mentioned earlier, we just love our rice and (are) not satisfied with just savoury dishes, we also love having it sweet. This particular rice dish is very tricky and my mother is convinced it was one of those recipes invented to test a daughter-in-law! Needless to say, I have never even tried it having been witness to several failed attempts of both my mother and my mother-in-law. However, it should not deter the brave, who after sampling this tasty delight, would undoubtedly prepare it again and again.

Ingredients

1 cup rice

2 tablespoons ghee (*toop*) + for serving

2-4 cloves

1½ -2 cups sugar

2-3 saffron threads

1 teaspoon powdered cardamom

6-7 almonds, soaked, peeled and slivered

1 tablespoon raisins

Method

- Wash the rice and set aside for 1 hour.
- Heat the ghee in a pressure cooker and gently fry the cloves.
- Add the rice and sauté for 2-3 minutes till the grains turn opaque.
- Add 2 cups of warm water and cook in a pressure cooker till the pressure is released twice (2 whistles). Allow the pressure to fall.
- Remove the lid and add the sugar, ½ cup of water, saffron and cardamom powder. Pressure cook again till the pressure is released once (1 whistle).
- Serve hot, sprinkled with dollops of ghee, almonds and raisins on top.

Note: For that extra zing, add a teaspoon of lime juice and/or 2 tablespoons freshly grated coconut. Another famous rice dish is *kesari bhaat*. I never really could differentiate between *kesari bhaat* and *saakhar bhaat* and perhaps the names are interchangeable as *kesar* is added to *saakhar bhaat*.

Naarali Bhaat

COCONUT RICE

As a small child, this dessert used to be my all-time favourite, especially since it was prepared on Coconut Day (*Naarali Poornima*). Coconut Day meant goodbye wet and rainy days, and welcome to a new season of feasting and merry-making. Along with coconut *barfi* and coconut *karanji*, this was a dish much relished and longed for. Unfortunately, this dish too is on its way to becoming extinct, thanks to the many diet programmes and healthy heart and diabetic associations!

Ingredients

1 cup rice

2 tablespoons ghee (*toop*)+ for serving

4-5 cloves

1 cup freshly grated coconut

1½ cups grated jaggery

1 teaspoon powdered cardamom

¼ cup raisins

Method

- Wash the rice, drain and set aside for at least 1 hour.
- Heat the ghee in a pressure cooker and fry the cloves.
- Add the rice and fry well.
- Add 2 cups of warm water, cover and cook till the pressure is released twice (2 whistles).
- Combine the coconut and jaggery and add to the rice. Cover and pressure cook till the pressure is released once (1 whistle).
- Remove the lid and stir in the powdered cardamom and raisins and some extra ghee.

Ambyacha Bhaat

MANGO RICE

Kokanasthas have a special weakness for Alphonso mangoes. My mother-in-law for one gets visibly upset when a guest refuses to eat a *hapoos* and looks upon him or her as a philistine. I digress a bit, but even today, on a hot summer day I can recall that loud wail of '*happoooos*!' in the street as the mango seller walks up and down with crates of mango balanced on his head. In the good old days when summer meant a holiday from school and a house full of children, with mangoes ripening faster than you could eat them, making mango pulp was a good way of keeping the little ones and their busy hands out of mischief, while at the same time making full use of nature's overflowing bounty. Huge amounts of *aamras* were consumed twice and some times thrice a day on the pretext that the rich orange colour of mango contained nutrients that helped you fight disease effectively for the rest of the year. And in keeping with the thrifty *Kokanastha* housewife, the unconsumed pulp was heated on a slow simmer till it became one thick lump of toffee, preserving all the sweetness of the fruit. This mango toffee was combined with evaporated milk (*khava*) to make the simply divine *ambyachi barfi* successfully marketed into worldwide fame by the Chitales of Pune.

For true aficionados of the Alphonso mango, who simply cannot get enough of the fruit, this rice dish is essential for an ideal summer lunch, especially when the market is flooded with its rich, inescapable and tantalisingly, tempting aroma.

Ingredients

1 cup rice
2 tablespoons ghee (*toop*)
2-3 cloves
1 cup mango pulp
½ cup sugar or to taste (optional)

Method

- Wash and drain the rice and set aside for 1 hour.
- In a pan, heat the ghee, cloves and rice. Fry until the rice turns opaque.
- Stir in 2 cups of warm water, the mango pulp and sugar and cook under pressure till the pressure is released twice (2 whistles).
- Remove from heat and serve. Needless to say this dessert is sticky, but delicious.

Note: These days, fruit like pineapple and even oranges are used to make fruit-flavoured, exotic sweet rice. However, with more and more people avoiding desserts, sweet rice as a main dish is highly unlikely to appear on a menu today. *Ambyacha bhaat* is particularly made for *Ashaadh Pathi*.

Dal, Aamti, Saar, Rassa, Kadhi ani Pithla

LENTILS AND CURRIES

Despite the irresistible fragrance of Ambemohar, plain steamed rice can be boring so we are lucky to have a wide range of accompaniments to complement it. On a hot day rice can be eaten with *dahi* or a simple light *kadhi*. On a wet, rainy day nothing can beat rice with a piping hot *rassa* and my all time, quick-fix meal of *pithla bhaat*.

Phodnicha Varan

SEASONED SPLIT PIGEON PEA CURRY

A slightly more grown-up variation of *varan* is *phodnicha varan* where a simple *phodni* (seasoning) of a few curry leaves, chopped tomato and chopped coriander are added and allowed to simmer for a while. Those who like a little zing to their food can add a slit green chilli as well. The dish is garnished with grated coconut and a pinch of sugar or a bit of jaggery.

Ingredients

1 teaspoon oil
¼ teaspoon mustard seeds
2 curry leaves
1 tomato, finely chopped
1 green chilli, slit
1 recipe Varan (page 34)
1 teaspoon finely chopped coriander
1 tablespoon freshly grated coconut
A pinch of sugar or grated jaggery (optional)

Method

- Heat the oil in a pan, and add the mustard seeds. When they start to splutter, add the curry leaves and lower the heat.
- Add the chopped tomato and green chilli. Stir and cook till tomato softens slightly. Add the cooked *varan* and simmer for 2 minutes.
- Serve hot, garnished with chopped coriander, grated coconut and a pinch of sugar.

Aamti

LENTIL CURRY

This humble *dal* is an acquired taste and is the ultimate test of a true Maharashtrian. Its sweet and sour taste is not universally palatable; so he who cannot eat *aamti* cannot be a true Maharashtrian.

Ingredients

1 cup split pigeon peas (*toor dal*)
¼ teaspoon turmeric powder
1 teaspoon Goda Masala (page 24, 25)
1½ tablespoons tamarind pulp
or 2-3 *kokum* rinds
A generous lump of jaggery
2 tablespoons finely chopped coriander
2 tablespoons freshly grated coconut

Seasoning

1 teaspoon oil
¼ teaspoon mustard seeds
2-3 curry leaves
A pinch of asafoetida (*hing*)
¼ teaspoon turmeric powder
¼ teaspoon red chilli powder
1 green chilli, chopped

Method

- Wash the pigeon peas. Drain. Place pigeon peas in a pressure cooker; add turmeric powder and 2½ cups of water and cook till the pressure is released 4 times (4 whistles). Mash the cooked *dal* with a *ravi* or the back of a ladle until smooth.
- For the seasoning, heat the oil in a separate pan and add mustard seeds, curry leaves, asafoetida, turmeric powder, chilli powder and green chilli and sauté till the seeds begin to splutter. Lower the heat and add the mashed *dal* to the seasoning.
- Add *goda masala*, tamarind pulp and the jaggery to counterbalance the sourness, and bring to a boil. Serve hot, garnished with chopped coriander and grated coconut.

Note: The amount of seasoning and the consistency of *aamti* depend on individual taste. Thus, you will find that it varies from family to family, and even from pot to pot. Unless you take a weighing scale and exactly measure out the amount of water that goes into the tamarind pulp or the amount of jaggery that goes into the *aamti*, there is bound to be a marginal variation and regular *aamti*-lovers can spot the difference. *Aamti* can be jazzed up with different vegetables of your choice to make it that much healthier and wholesome. Commonly used vegetables are cauliflower and French beans, but what is really typical is *vaangyache varan*.

Vaangyache Varan

LENTILS WITH BRINJAL

Ingredients

1 cup split pigeon peas (*toor dal*)
1 cup quartered small brinjals
1 teaspoon Goda Masala (page 24, 25)
1 tablespoon tamarind pulp or 2-3 *kokum* rinds
A small piece of jaggery
Grated coconut, for garnishing
Chopped coriander, for garnishing

Seasoning

1 teaspoon oil
¼ teaspoon mustard seeds
2-3 curry leaves
A pinch of asafoetida (*hing*)
¼ teaspoon turmeric powder
¼ teaspoon red chilli powder
1 green chilli, chopped

Method

- Wash the pigeon peas. Drain.
- Place the pigeon peas in a pressure cooker, and add 2½ cups of water and cook till the pressure is released 4 times (4 whistles).
- Mash the *dal* with a *ravi* or the back of a ladle until smooth.
- For the seasoning, heat the oil in a pan and add mustard seeds, curry leaves, asafoetida, turmeric powder, chilli powder and green chilli. Add the brinjals and fry for 2 minutes.
- Add the mashed *dal*, *goda masala*, tamarind pulp, and jaggery, and bring to a boil. Lower heat and cook till the brinjals are soft.
- Garnish with grated coconut and chopped coriander.

Paalakchi Dal

LENTILS WITH SPINACH

Ingredients

1 cup (200g) split pigeon peas (*toor dal*)

2½ cups chopped spinach

¼ teaspoon turmeric powder

1 teaspoon Goda Masala (page 24, 25)

1 tablespoon tamarind pulp or 2-3 *kokum* rinds

A small piece of jaggery

Seasoning

1 teaspoon oil

¼ teaspoon mustard seeds

2-3 curry leaves

A pinch of asafoetida (*hing*)

¼ teaspoon turmeric powder

¼ teaspoon red chilli powder

1 green chilli, chopped

Method

- Wash the pigeon peas. Drain.
- Place pigeon peas in a pressure cooker, add the chopped spinach, turmeric powder and 2½ cups of water and cook till the pressure is released 4 times (four whistles).
- Mash the *dal* with a *ravi* or the back of a ladle, until smooth.
- For the seasoning, heat the oil in a pan and add mustard seeds, curry leaves, asafoetida, turmeric powder, chilli powder and chopped green chilli.
- Add the mashed *dal* mixture, *goda masala*, tamarind pulp and jaggery to taste. Bring to a boil.
- Serve hot with Bhaat (page 35) or Poli (page 130).

Note: The amount of spinach can be reduced to 1 cup if you don't like your *dal* too spinachy!

Methichi Dal

LENTILS WITH FENUGREEK LEAVES

Ingredients

1 cup split pigeon peas (*toor dal*)
1 cup chopped fenugreek leaves
¼ teaspoon fenugreek seeds
½ cup peanuts
1 teaspoon Goda Masala (page 24, 25)
1 tablespoon tamarind pulp
or 3-4 *kokum* rinds
1 tablespoon jaggery, or to taste

Seasoning

1 teaspoon oil
¼ teaspoon mustard seeds
2-3 curry leaves
A pinch of asafoetida (*hing*)
¼ teaspoon turmeric powder
1 teaspoon red chilli powder
1 green chilli, chopped

Method

- Wash the pigeon peas. Drain.
- Place pigeon peas in a pressure cooker, add the chopped fenugreek, fenugreek seeds, peanuts and 2½ cups of water and cook till the pressure is released 4 times (4 whistles). Mash the *dal* mixture with a *ravi* or the back of a ladle until smooth.
- For the seasoning, heat the oil in a pan and add mustard seeds, curry leaves, asafoetida, turmeric powder, chilli powder and chopped green chilli.
- Add the mashed *dal* mixture, *goda masala*, tamarind pulp, and jaggery.
- Bring to the boil and serve with Bhaat (page 35) and Poli (page 130) or *chapati*.

Tomatoche Saar – I

SPICY TOMATO COCONUT CURRY-I

Made with tomato and coconut, this light yet delicately flavoured curry is my personal favourite. Perhaps it is due to my mother's penchant for serving this at parties when she was looking for something particularly different and exotic. One evening she audaciously served this curry as a soup, much to the delight of her unsuspecting guests. Its sweet and sour flavour enhanced by the seasoning was much appreciated by all that night.

Ingredients

¼ kg ripe tomatoes, chopped
¼ beetroot, chopped
½ cup freshly grated coconut
½ cup sugar or to taste
2 teaspoons salt or to taste
2 tablespoons chopped coriander

Spice paste

2-3 garlic cloves
1 inch ginger
¼ teaspoon cumin powder
5-6 green chillies

Method

- In a pressure cooker, cook the tomatoes and beetroot in 1½ cups of water till the pressure is released 3 times (3 whistles) or till soft and pulpy.
- Pureé the mixture in a blender. The beetroot adds to the rich colour of the saar, which can otherwise remain a pasty orange.
- Grind the coconut and extract the milk (approximately 1 cup), or 200 ml packaged coconut milk.
- To make the spice paste, grind together the garlic, ginger, cumin powder and green chillies.
- Strain the tomato-beetroot purée. Add the coconut milk and spice paste to the strained liquid and stir well.
- Add the sugar and salt, and gently bring to a boil to prevent the coconut milk from curdling. Serve, garnished with chopped coriander.

Note: This *saar* is normally served at room temperature as frequent reheating will cause it to curdle.

Tomatoche Saar – II

SPICY TOMATO COCONUT CURRY-II

An alternative recipe that has been devised by my mother is given below:

Ingredients

¼ kg ripe tomatoes, chopped
¼ beetroot
1 cup buttermilk
½ cup sugar
2 teaspoons salt or to taste
Chopped fresh coriander, for garnishing

Seasoning

1 tablespoon ghee (*toop*)
2-3 curry leaves
5-6 green chillies
1 inch ginger, finely chopped
¼ teaspoon cumin powder

Method

- In a pressure cooker, cook the tomatoes and beetroot in 1 cup of water till the pressure is released twice (2 whistles), or till soft and pulpy.
- Pureé the mixture in a blender.
- Add the buttermilk to the purée and blend until smooth.
- For the seasoning, heat ghee in a pan and add curry leaves, green chillies, ginger, and cumin powder.
- Add the buttermilk-tomato mixture, sugar and salt to taste and bring to a boil on low heat to prevent it from curdling.
- Serve at room temperature, garnished with chopped coriander.

Golyachi Aamti

LENTIL DUMPLING CURRY

Ingredients

2 cups split pigeon peas (*toor dal*)
1 teaspoon cumin seeds
1 teaspoon coriander seeds
4-5 green chillies
Salt to taste
1 teaspoon + 2 cups oil for deep-frying
½ teaspoon mustard seeds
½ teaspoon turmeric powder
2-3 curry leaves
1 teaspoon Goda Masala (page 24, 25)
1 tablespoon jaggery
2-3 *kokum* rinds
2 tablespoons grated dried coconut
1 tablespoon chopped coriander

Method

- Wash, and soak the pigeon peas for 2 hours. Drain.
- Grind the pigeon peas to make a very thick doughy batter.
- Grind the cumin seeds, ½ teaspoon coriander seeds and green chillies together. Add to the batter and mix well. Add salt to taste. Mix well and set aside.
- Divide the mixture into small lime-sized balls (*gola*).
- Heat 2 cups of oil in a *kadai* and deep-fry the balls until golden brown. Set aside.
- Heat 1 teaspoon oil in a pan; and the mustard seeds, turmeric powder, curry leaves, and *goda masala*.
- Add 2 cups of water, salt, jaggery and *kokum* rinds.
- Grind the dried coconut and remaining coriander seeds together and add to the pan; mix well and bring the mixture to a boil.
- Add the fried dumplings to the boiling mixture, lower the heat, and simmer for another 5 minutes.
- Garnish with chopped coriander and serve.

Katachi Aamti

SWEET AND SOUR THIN LENTIL CURRY

This curry is normally made with *kat* - the water that is drained from split Bengal gram (*chana dal*) cooked to make *puran poli*. It is also eaten with the *puran poli* and is the perfect foil to its sweetness.

Ingredients

A lemon-sized ball of tamarind

8 cups of *kat* (the water that is drained off from the cooked *chana dal*)

½ cup jaggery

2 teaspoons red chilli powder

2 teaspoons salt

¼ cup grated dried coconut

1 teaspoon cumin seeds

1 teaspoon Goda Masala (page 24, 25)

1 tablespoon finely chopped coriander

1 tablespoon freshly grated coconut (optional)

Seasoning

1 teaspoon oil

¼ teaspoon mustard seeds

¼ teaspoon turmeric powder

2-3 curry leaves

Method

- Soak the tamarind in ½ cup of water for 10 minutes. Then squeeze out the pulp and add to the *kat*. Add the jaggery, chilli powder and salt and mix well.
- Heat a *tawa*, and dry-roast the dried coconut and cumin seeds together. Grind to a paste. Set aside.
- For the seasoning, heat the oil in a pan and add the mustard seeds, turmeric powder and curry leaves and fry till the mustard seeds splutter.
- Add the *goda masala* and ground coconut paste and stir.
- Add the *kat*, 1 cup of water and bring to a boil.
- Garnish with chopped coriander and serve.

Note: The consistency of this curry is like that of a thick soup. Some people like to add chopped drumstick pods to this curry. Cut 2 drumstick pods into 2-inch long pieces and add to the pan after the seasoning. Once the drumstick pods are half cooked, add the *kat*.

Amsulache Saar/Sol Kadhi

KOKUM CURRY

Going back to our Konkan heritage *amsulache saar* or *sol kadhi* is the best way to wash down a satisfying summer meal. Tinged a delicate pink, just a little sour and extremely exotic, the *kadhi* is made out of *amsul* or *kokum*, the dried rind of a variety of mangosteen.

The Kokum tree (*Garcinia indica*) grows all along the Konkan coast. The red berries have medicinal properties: the butter extracted from the pulp is used as a traditional ointment for chapped feet and to soothe burns. The rind of the fruit is sun-dried and used as a souring agent. An infusion of the rinds is an ideal antihistamine to treat allergies and skin rashes.

Ingredients

½ teaspoon ghee (*toop*)
½ teaspoon cumin seeds
5-6 dried kokum rinds (*aamsul*)
2 green chillies, finely chopped
2 cups coconut milk extracted from 1 coconut
Salt to taste
A small piece of jaggery
2 tablespoons chopped coriander

Method

- Heat ghee in a pan till it reaches smoking point. Lower the heat, and add cumin seeds.
- When the cumin seeds start to sizzle, add the *kokum* rinds, green chillies and 2 cups of water. Bring to a boil.
- Stir in the coconut milk, salt and jaggery to taste. Leave to cool.
- Remove the *kokum* rinds before serving, and sprinkle with chopped coriander.
- Serve at room temperature or chilled.

Kadhi

YOGHURT CURRY

The hallmark of a good *kadhi* is its consistency - it should be neither too thick nor too thin, nor too sour, but above all, it should be very smooth. Considering that most of the time *kadhi* is made from the buttermilk left over from making *toop*, it is extremely difficult to determine just how sour the buttermilk really is, and this is where the skill of the cook comes into play. This version has garlic added, which is how my father likes it. But you can leave it out to make a traditional *Kokanastha kadhi*.

Ingredients

2 cups buttermilk
1 teaspoon gram flour
Salt to taste
1 teaspoon ghee (*toop*)
½ teaspoon cumin seeds
2-3 curry leaves
1 inch ginger, finely chopped
1 green chilli, slit
4-5 cloves garlic (optional)
A pinch of sugar

Method

- In a bowl, mix the buttermilk with gram flour till smooth. Add salt to taste.
- Heat the ghee in a pan; add cumin seeds and curry leaves and sauté till they begin to sizzle.
- Add the ginger, green chilli and garlic and sauté for a minute.
- Lower the heat and stir in the buttermilk.
- Gently bring the *kadhi* to the boil, stirring continuously, to prevent it from curdling. Add a pinch of sugar.
- Serve hot, garnished with chopped fresh coriander.

Rassa

BASIC COCONUT CURRY

Rassa is a vegetable curry and is a good substitute for *dal*. The base of the curry is a spice paste to which vegetables of choice are added such as potatoes, cauliflower, peas, beans or mixed vegetables.

Ingredients

5 tablespoons Rassa Masala (see note)

1 tablespoon Goda Masala (page 24, 25)

1 cup chopped mix vegetables or any one vegetable of your choice

Salt to taste

Sugar to taste

1 tablespoon chopped fresh coriander

1 tablespoon grated fresh coconut

Seasoning

1 tablespoon oil

¼ teaspoon mustard seeds

¼ teaspoon asafoetida (*hing*)

¼ teaspoon turmeric powder

2-3 curry leaves

1 teaspoon red chilli powder (optional)

Method

- Heat the oil in pan and add the mustard seeds, when they begin to splutter, add the asafoetida, turmeric powder, curry leaves, and chilli powder.
- Add *rassa masala, goda masala* and the chopped vegetables.
- Mix well and add 1 cup of water, cook covered, on low heat till the vegetables are cooked.
- Add salt and sugar to taste.
- Serve garnished with chopped coriander and grated coconut.

Note: To make *rassa masala*, heat 2 tablespoons oil and fry 1 large (100 grams) finely chopped onion, till golden brown. Add 2 chopped garlic cloves, 1 inch ginger and ¾ cup (80 grams) freshly grated coconut and fry till brown. Add 1 tablespoon poppy seeds and sauté till golden. Remove from heat and leave to cool. Grind the spices into a fine paste.

Batatyacha Rassa

GRAVIED POTATOES

This simple gravied vegetable is always a crowd pleaser since it is made out of the ever popular potato.

Ingredients

2 teaspoons oil
½ teaspoon mustard seeds
¼ teaspoon asafoetida (*hing*)
¼ teaspoon cumin seeds
¼ teaspoon turmeric powder
2-3 curry leaves
1 cup chopped onion
½ teaspoon red chilli powder
½ cup chopped tomato
1 teaspoon Goda Masala (Page 24, 25)
1 cup peeled and chopped potatoes
2-3 *kokum* rinds
Salt to taste
A pinch of sugar
1 teaspoon chopped coriander
1 teaspoon freshly grated coconut

Spice Paste

2 tablespoons grated coconut
½ teaspoons cumin seeds
1 green chilli
½ inch ginger (optional)
2 cloves garlic (optional)

Method

- Grind together the ingredients for the spice paste. Set aside.
- Heat oil in a pan and add the mustard seeds, asafoetida, cumin seeds, and turmeric powder. Add the curry leaves, chopped onion and chilli powder.
- When the onion starts to brown, add the tomato, *goda masala* and spice paste and sauté until the oil separates. Add the chopped potatoes, and cook, stirring continuously, for 5 minutes.
- Lower the heat, add the *kokum*, salt and sufficient water to make a gravy. Cook, covered, on low heat, till the potatoes are tender. A pinch of sugar will balance the flavours of the gravy. Serve hot, garnished with chopped coriander and grated coconut.

Note: This *rassa* tastes equally good without onion, garlic and ginger!

Flower ani Batatyacha Rassa

GRAVIED CAULIFLOWER AND POTATOES

Cauliflowers, potatoes and tomatoes are perennial palate pleasers. Years ago a famous caterer in Pune named Dingankar was known for his *rassa*, and even today, the mere mention of this dish produces burps of appreciation, *Kokanastha* style!

Ingredients

2 teaspoons oil
¼ teaspoon mustard seeds
A pinch of asafoetida (*hing*)
¼ teaspoon cumin seeds
¼ teaspoon turmeric powder
½ teaspoon red chilli powder
2-3 curry leaves
1 cup chopped onion
½ cup grated tomato
1 teaspoon Goda Masala (page 24, 25)
1 cup cauliflower florets
1 cup peeled and chopped potatoes
2-3 *kokum* rinds
A pinch of sugar
1 teaspoon chopped coriander
1 teaspoon freshly grated coconut

Spice Paste

2 tablespoons grated coconut
½ teaspoons cumin seeds
1 green chilli
½ inch ginger (optional)
2 cloves garlic (optional)

Method

- Grind together the ingredients for the spice paste. Set aside.
- Heat oil in a pan and add mustard seeds, asafoetida, cumin seeds, turmeric powder and chilli powder.
- Add the grated tomato, *goda masala* and spice paste and sauté for a few minutes.
- Add the cauliflower florets and potatoes, and cook, stirring continuously, for 5 minutes.
- Lower the heat, and add the *kokum* and sufficient water to make a gravy. Cover and simmer till the vegetables are just tender. Add a pinch of sugar to the gravy. Garnish with chopped coriander and grated coconut.

Note: Add 1 cup fresh green peas to make this an even more delicious *rassa*!

Tomato ani Batatyacha Rassa

CURRIED POTATOES AND TOMATOES

Ingredients

2 teaspoons oil
½ teaspoon mustard seeds
¼ teaspoon asafoetida (*hing*)
¼ teaspoon cumin seeds
½ teaspoon turmeric powder
½ teaspoon red chilli powder
2-3 curry leaves
1 cup chopped onion
1 cup grated tomato
1 teaspoon Goda Masala (page 24, 25)
1 cup (1-inch long) potato straws
½ cup chopped tomato
2-3 *kokum* rinds
A pinch of sugar
1 teaspoon chopped coriander
1 teaspoon freshly grated coconut

Spice Paste

2 tablespoons grated coconut
½ teaspoon cumin seeds
1 green chilli
½ inch ginger (optional)
2 cloves garlic (optional)

Method

- Grind together the ingredients for the spice paste. Set aside.
- Heat the oil in a pan and add mustard seeds, asafoetida, cumin seeds, turmeric powder and chilli powder.
- Add the curry leaves and chopped onion and sauté till the onions turn brown.
- Add the grated tomato, *goda masala* and spice paste, and sauté for a few minutes.
- Add the potato straws and chopped tomato, and cook, stirring continuously, for 5 minutes.
- Lower the heat and add *kokum* and sufficient water to make a gravy. Cover and simmer till the potatoes are just tender.
- Add a pinch of sugar to the gravy.
- Serve hot, garnished with chopped coriander and grated coconut.

Pithla

GRAM FLOUR CURRY

Traditionally eaten at the end of the wedding festivities, this absolutely delicious gram flour curry is the first resort of the lazy cook. This is a never-fail recipe because it is simply perfect on a rainy, wet day or a cold, winter night, especially when eaten with Bhaakri (page 133) or Bhaat (page 35).

Ingredients

1 teaspoon oil
¼ teaspoon mustard seeds
¼ teaspoon turmeric powder
½ teaspoon red chilli powder
1 small onion, chopped (optional)
½ teaspoon chopped garlic (optional)
1-2 green chillies, chopped
Salt to taste
1-2 *kokum* rinds
½ cup gram flour

Method

- Heat oil in a *kadai*, and add the mustard seeds, turmeric powder, and chilli powder.
- Add the onion and garlic and fry until soft, and then add 1 cup of water.
- Add chopped green chillies, and bring to a boil. Add salt and *kokum*.
- Lower the heat and add the gram flour, stirring continuously, to make sure no lumps are formed.
- Cook, covered, until the gram flour is cooked. Serve hot.

Note: I like my *pithla* to be teary-eye spicy with the consistency of custard. I also like to eat it with *danyache koot*, which is coarsely pounded roasted peanuts. Some people do not like the onions while others like to add a generous amount of garlic. So you see how a simple dish can be made in several ways to ensure that your *pithla* is unique to your table. Incidentally, a very dry *pithla* becomes *jhunka*. A special tip I'd like to share is that *pithla* made in the regular *kadai* is mind blowing as compared to that made in a non-stick pan, so for that authentic just-like-grannymade-it taste, look for the old fashioned heavy iron *kadai* that must be languishing in some attic somewhere.

Bhaajya

VEGETABLE DISHES

Bhaaji is a generic term to describe a side dish of seasonal vegetables. Leafy greens should be avoided in rainy weather when huge clumps of mud stick to the roots. It is only common sense to wash the vegetables thoroughly to ensure that there are no creepy crawlies or hidden organisms that can cause a runny tummy or worse. After the vegetable is chopped, it is added to the pot of sizzling *phodni* with a dash of magic *masala*. With salt added to taste and a good stir, it is left to simmer in a covered pan till tender. Most vegetables cook in their own juices and do not require any additional water.

Depending on the type of vegetable to be cooked, one can add 1-2 teaspoons of *goda masala* after the vegetables are added to the seasoning. To spice things up a bit, this simple formula can be modified with chopped green chillies, or any other spices such as powdered coriander and cumin seeds. For good measure, a pinch of sugar or a bit of jaggery is always added to give it that smooth, perfect finish. To ensure that vegetables are evenly cooked, some water should be left to evaporate on the lid of the pan to ensure that the vegetables cook at the top as well. Bitter beans particularly require the jaggery to offset their slightly bitter taste. Care should be taken not to overcook the *bhaaji* (unless of course you prefer them to be squishy), and should be finished off with a generous sprinkling of freshly grated coconut and chopped coriander before serving.

CUTTING VEGETABLES

Before I go on to the actual recipes for the different vegetables, I would like to mention how important it is to cut the vegetables just right. Obviously a potato is a potato is a potato, but the way it is cut affects the taste. It is, therefore important to pay attention to how the vegetable should be cut.

Potatoes can be made into *kachrya* or thin slices, by quartering the potato lengthwise, and then making fine slices out of each potato chip. They can also be quartered and then halved to get bite-sized pieces.

Ivy gourd can be quartered lengthwise or sliced into thin round slices.

Ladies' fingers can be halved and quartered lengthwise or cut into bite-sized pieces. They can also be slit lengthwise and stuffed with *masala* paste.

French beans can be cut horizontally into rings or diagonally into thin slices.

Batatyache Kachrya

SPICED POTATO

Almost the first *bhaaji* a young girl learns to make is the evergreen, ever popular *batatyache kachrya*. *Kachrya* actually means thin fine slices. Most often the potato is sliced with the skin on, which adds to the flavour and nutritiousness of this otherwise calorie-laden *bhaaji*.

Ingredients

¼ kg potatoes
Salt to taste
A pinch of sugar
A dash of lime juice
1 teaspoon freshly grated coconut
1 teaspoon chopped coriander

Seasoning

1 teaspoon oil
2-3 curry leaves
¼ teaspoon mustard seeds
A pinch of asafoetida (*hing*)
¼ teaspoon turmeric powder
½ teaspoon red chilli powder

Method

- Quarter the potatoes and then cut them into thin slices.
- For the seasoning, heat the oil in a pan and add the curry leaves, mustard seeds, asafoetida, turmeric powder and chilli powder.
- When the seeds begin to splutter, add the potatoes and mix.
- Sprinkle just a little water and salt. Lower the heat, cover and simmer for 5 minutes. A small quantity of water on the lid makes the *bhaaji* cook that much faster without the excess water.
- To test if the potatoes are tender, pierce the potato with a fork or the point of a knife. It should slide in smoothly when cooked.
- Add a pinch of sugar and a dash of lime juice and mix. Garnish with grated coconut and chopped coriander and serve with Puri (page 132).

Note: This *bhaaji* is everyone's favourite food for picnics or long journeys, or on days when you need to rustle up something in a jiffy.

Farazbichi Bhaaji

SPICED FRENCH BEANS

When I was a little girl we spent a few years in Pune where we had a small kitchen garden. I remember running out in the drizzling rain and picking French beans that had grown long enough to be eaten. I have never eaten such tender, tasty beans.

Ingredients

¼ kg French beans
2 medium potatoes or
½ cup shelled peas
Salt to taste
1 teaspoon freshly grated coconut
1 teaspoon chopped coriander
A pinch of sugar
A dash of lime juice

Seasoning

1 teaspoon oil
2-3 curry leaves
¼ teaspoon mustard seeds
A pinch of asafoetida (*hing*)
¼ teaspoon turmeric powder
½ teaspoon red chilli powder

Method

- Chop the beans diagonally or horizontally into thin slices. It may seem strange, but the way the beans are cut actually affects the way they taste, the diagonally chopped ones seem to taste better!
- For the seasoning, heat the oil in a pan, and add the curry leaves, mustard seeds, asafoetida, turmeric powder and *goda masala*.
- Add the potatoes and mix. Add salt, and sprinkle a little water. Lower the heat, cover the pan and leave to cook for 2 minutes.
- When the potatoes are soft, add the beans, *goda masala* and jaggery, and mix well.
- Add 2-3 tablespoons more water and cook, covered, for 2-3 minutes, till the beans are tender.
- Serve, garnished with grated coconut and chopped.

Note: This recipe can be used to make *bhaaji* of other beans like the flat broad beans (*papdi*), which is shelled, the two halves of the pods separated, and broken into bite-sized pieces.

Gavar ani Batatyachi Bhaaji

SPICED CLUSTER BEANS WITH POTATOES

Perhaps the slightly sweetish taste in our food makes us enjoy vegetables that are bitter! Indeed, one of my favourites is this simple dish made with cluster beans or *gavar*. In the monsoon, when this bean is in season, it is tender and fresh, and is delightful when teamed up with potatoes.

Ingredients

2 medium potatoes

Salt to taste

¼ kg cluster beans (*gavar*), broken into 1-inch pieces

1 teaspoon Goda Masala (page 24, 25)

A small lump of jaggery

1 teaspoon freshly grated coconut

1 teaspoon chopped coriander

Seasoning

1 teaspoon oil

2-3 curry leaves

¼ teaspoon mustard seeds

¼ teaspoon turmeric powder

½ teaspoon red chilli powder

¼ teaspoon asafoetida (*hing*)

Method

- Peel the potatoes. Quarter them and cut into half-inch cubes.
- For the seasoning, heat oil in a pan and add the curry leaves, mustard seeds, turmeric powder, chilli powder and asafoetida.
- Add the potatoes and mix. Add salt, and sprinkle a little water. Lower the heat, cover the pan and leave to cook for 2 minutes.
- When the potatoes are soft, add the beans, *goda masala* and jaggery, and mix well.
- Add 2-3 tablespoons more water and cook, covered, for 2-3 minutes, till the beans are tender.
- Serve, garnished with grated coconut and chopped coriander.

Note: This *bhaaji* is just as tasty without the potato!

Flowerchi Bhaaji

SPICED CAULIFLOWER

Ingredients

2 medium potatoes, cut into ½-inch cubes

¼ kg cauliflower, separated into small florets

Salt to taste

1 teaspoon freshly grated coconut

1 teaspoon chopped coriander

A pinch of sugar or a small lump of jaggery

Seasoning

1 teaspoon oil

2-3 curry leaves

¼ teaspoon mustard seeds

¼ teaspoon asafoetida (*hing*)

½ teaspoon turmeric powder

½ teaspoon red chilli powder

1 teaspoon Goda Masala (page 24, 25)

Method

- For the seasoning, heat the oil in a pan and add the curry leaves, mustard seeds, asafoetida, turmeric powder, chilli powder and *goda masala*.
- Add the potatoes and cook for 5 minutes till almost tender.
- Add the cauliflower and mix well. Add 2-3 tablespoons of water, salt, grated coconut, chopped coriander, and a pinch of sugar. Cover and cook on low heat for 5 minutes.
- Serve hot with Poli (page 130).

Note: This *bhaaji* can be made without potatoes and can also be cooked in milk instead of water, which gives it a unique, creamy flavour.

Kobichi Bhaaji

SPICED CABBAGE

Deceptively simple, cooking a good cabbage *bhaaji* is quite an art. There is a very thin line between plain boiled cabbage and a lip-smacking vegetable. So be warned that this *bhaaji* is not as simple as it looks!

Ingredients

¼ kg cabbage, finely chopped
Salt to taste
1 teaspoon freshly grated coconut
1 teaspoon chopped coriander

Seasoning

1 teaspoon oil
2-3 curry leaves
¼ teaspoon mustard seeds
A pinch of asafoetida (*hing*)
¼ teaspoon turmeric powder
1 green chilli, finely chopped

Method

- For the seasoning, heat the oil in a pan and add the curry leaves, mustard seeds, asafoetida, turmeric powder, and chopped green chillies.
- Add the cabbage and mix well. Add 2-3 tablespoons of water, salt, grated coconut and chopped coriander.
- Cook, covered, on low heat for 5 minutes, until tender.
- Serve hot with Poli (page 130).

Note: This *bhaaji* can also be made with potato in which case 1 potato should be enough for ¼ kg cabbage. My favourite form of *kobichi bhaaji* is one which has either fresh green peas or a handful of soaked split Bengal gram added to it. In either case, the peas or *dal* should be added to the seasoning, allowed to cook for a while before adding the cabbage. Most people like this *bhaaji* green and crunchy in which case it is advisable to omit the turmeric powder and cook the *bhaaji* for just about 2 minutes.

Dodkyachi Bhaaji

SPICED RIDGE GOURD

Ingredients

¼ cup split Bengal gram (*chana dal*)
¼ kg ridge gourd
Salt to taste
1 teaspoon grated coconut
1 teaspoon chopped coriander

Seasoning

1 teaspoon oil
2-3 curry leaves
¼ teaspoon mustard seeds
½ teaspoon turmeric powder
½ teaspoon red chilli powder
A pinch of asafoetida (*hing*)

Method

- Wash and soak the split Bengal gram for 10 minutes.
- Peel the ridge gourd, and cut it lengthwise, and chop into bite-sized pieces.
- For the seasoning, heat the oil in a pan, and add curry leaves, mustard seeds, turmeric powder, chilli powder, and asafoetida.
- Add the split Bengal gram, stir well and lower the heat.
- Add the chopped vegetable and salt and mix well.
- Cover and allow to simmer till the gram is soft.
- Remove from heat and garnish with grated coconut and chopped coriander.

Padwalchi Bhaaji

SPICED SNAKE GOURD

If you have ever wondered what this long snake-like vegetable tastes like, I assure you this is the best introduction to this bhaaji. Quick and easy to make, I was quite astounded when my husband's uncle asked for the recipe. I thought it was popular in every home till he corrected me: normally people eat it stuffed with a vegetable or potato filling. It appeared I was the only one who liked it this way, cooked with gram flour.

Ingredients

½ cup split Bengal gram (*chana dal*)

¼ kg snake gourd (*padwal/chachinda*)

Salt to taste

1 teaspoon freshly grated coconut

1 teaspoon chopped coriander

Seasoning

1 teaspoon oil

2-3 curry leaves

¼ teaspoon mustard seeds

¼ teaspoon turmeric powder

½ teaspoon red chilli powder

A pinch of asafoetida (*hing*)

Method

- Wash and soak split Bengal gram for 10 minutes.
- Peel the snake gourd; cut it lengthwise, remove the seeds and chop into ¼-inch thick slices.
- For the seasoning, heat the oil in a pan and add curry leaves, mustard seeds, turmeric powder, chilli powder and asafoetida.
- Stir well and lower the heat. Add the snake gourd, soaked split Bengal gram, and salt and stir well.
- Cook, covered, on low heat, till the *dal* is soft.
- Remove from heat and serve, garnished with grated coconut and chopped coriander.

Note: You can use gram flour instead of split Bengal gram. Prepare the seasoning, add the ridge gourd and salt, cover and allow the vegetable to sweat. Add as much gram flour as will be absorbed (about ½ cup), stirring continuously, till the gram flour is cooked. Take off the heat and serve without any garnish.

Tondlichi Bhaaji

CURRIED IVY GOURD

While this is not my favourite *bhaaji*, we land up eating it at least three times a week, as it is one of the few *bhaaji* my husband eats without making a fuss. This tiny green gherkin like vegetable is available all year round and can be cooked simply to a slight crisp, or jazzed up with a *masala* stuffing and served as a special *bhaaji*.

Ingredients

¼ kg ivy gourd (*tondli*)
Salt to taste
1 teaspoon freshly grated coconut
1 teaspoon chopped coriander

Seasoning

1 teaspoon oil
2-3 curry leaves
¼ teaspoon mustard seeds
A pinch of asafoetida (*hing*)
¼ teaspoon turmeric powder
1 green chilli, finely chopped

Method

- Chop the ivy gourd into thin round slices, or lengthwise into thin slices.
- For the seasoning, heat the oil in a pan and add curry leaves, mustard seeds, asafoetida, turmeric powder and green chilli.
- Add the chopped vegetable and mix together. Add 2-3 tablespoons of water, cover and simmer for 5 minutes.
- When the *bhaaji* is almost tender, add the salt.
- Sprinkle with coconut and chopped coriander and serve hot.

Note: Some people like their ivy gourd crisp and this can only be done when it is finely sliced. Also it tastes better when it is slightly oilier, so you could increase the oil to 1 tablespoon.

Bhendichi Bhaaji

SPICED LADIES' FINGERS

Bhendi evokes strong reactions. Either you like them or you don't. For those who like this bhaaji, ¼ kg is not enough (the vegetable shrinks when it is cooked so ½ kg will just about yield enough for a family of four.

Ingredients

¼ kg ladies' fingers (*bhendi*)
1 teaspoon grated coconut
1 teaspoon chopped coriander

Seasoning

1 teaspoon oil
2-3 curry leaves
¼ teaspoon mustard seeds
A pinch of asafoetida (*hing*)
½ teaspoon turmeric powder
1 green chilli, finely chopped

Method

- Chop the ladies' fingers into ½ -inch pieces.
- For the seasoning, heat the oil in a pan and add the curry leaves, mustard seeds, asafoetida, turmeric powder, and chillies.
- Add the ladies' fingers and mix well. Cover the pan with a lid and pour some water on top. Cook on low heat, for 5 minutes.
- When the *bhaaji* is almost tender, add the salt.
- Garnish with grated coconut and chopped coriander and serve.

Note: Do not add any water to this dish while cooking as it becomes sticky.

Navalkohlachi Bhaaji

SPICED KOHLRABI

This turnip-like vegetable is available in the winter, but one should be careful as an old kohlrabi can be stringy and quite annoying, especially when the stringy bits get stuck between the teeth!

Ingredients

¼ kg tender kohlrabi (*navalkohl*)
2 tablespoons water or milk or coconut milk
Salt to taste
1 teaspoon freshly grated coconut
1 teaspoon chopped coriander

Seasoning

1 teaspoon oil
2-3 curry leaves
¼ teaspoon mustard seeds
A pinch of asafoetida (*hing*)
¼ teaspoon turmeric powder
1 green chilli, finely chopped

Method

- Peel the outer skin of the kohlrabi and cut into half, cut into wedges and then into 1-inch pieces. For the seasoning, heat the oil in a pan and add the curry leaves, mustard seeds, asafoetida, turmeric powder and chillies.
- Add the kohlrabi and give it a good stir. Add 2 tablespoons of water cover and simmer for 5 minutes.
- When the *bhaaji* is almost tender, add salt.
- Garnish with the coconut and chopped coriander and serve.

Note: This *bhaaji* tastes particularly delicious when you add ½ cup shelled green peas.

Fansachi Bhaaji

SPICED JACKFRUIT

This is probably the ugliest fruit in the universe, but unbelievably tasty. Care should be taken to cook jackfruit that is very unripe and green of the *kappa* variety, and not of the *barka* variety.

Ingredients

5 cashew nuts
1 tablespoon shelled peanuts
½ kg unripe jackfruit
Salt to taste
1 teaspoon grated coconut
1 teaspoon chopped coriander

Seasoning

1 teaspoon oil
2-3 curry leaves
¼ teaspoon mustard seeds
A pinch of asafoetida (*hing*)
¼ teaspoon turmeric powder
1 dried red chilli, finely chopped

Method

- Soak the cashew nuts and peanuts for 10 minutes.
- Remove the hard outer skin of the jackfruit with either a well-greased knife, or better still a *vili* (page 21).
- Chop the jackfruit into 1-inch pieces and remove the seeds.
- Remove the tough outer skin of the seeds and use the seeds in the *bhaaji*.
- For the seasoning, heat the oil and add the curry leaves, mustard seeds, asafoetida, turmeric powder and dried chilli.
- Add the jackfruit, cashew nuts and peanuts, and give it a good stir.
- Add 2 tablespoons of water, cover and simmer for 10 minutes.
- When the *bhaaji* is almost tender, add salt.
- Garnish with grated coconut and chopped coriander and serve hot.

Note: A special garlic seasoning can be prepared by sautéing 2-3 crushed cloves of garlic and 2 dried red chillies in 2 tablespoons of hot oil.

Kelfulachi Bhaaji

SPICED BANANA FLOWER

Yes, you heard right, even banana flowers can be made into a *bhaaji*. Unfortunately this very tasty *bhaaji* is given short shrift largely because of the labour involved in making it: you have to be very careful to remove the tiny pistil inside the tinier flower which is nestled in between the layers of red banana leaves.

Ingredients

1 banana flower
2 tablespoons sour buttermilk or
a small piece of tamarind, soaked in water
½ cup split Bengal gram (*chana dal*)
Salt to taste
1 teaspoon cumin powder
Jaggery to taste
Grated dried coconut to taste
2 teaspoons chopped coriander

Seasoning

1 tablespoon oil
¼ teaspoon mustard seeds
A pinch of asafoetida (*hing*)
¼ teaspoon turmeric powder
½ teaspoon red chilli powder

Method

- Gently peel the banana flower and remove the white flowers nestled inside. Remove and discard the stamen and pistil. Finely chop the flowers and soak them in the sour buttermilk or tamarind water for 5-6 hours.
- Soak the split Bengal gram in water.
- Drain the chopped banana flower, and boil in salted water.
- For the seasoning, heat the oil in a *kadai* and add the mustard seeds. When they start to splutter add the asafoetida, turmeric powder and chilli powder.
- Drain the chopped banana flower and add it to the seasoning. Stir to mix.
- Add salt, cumin powder, jaggery and grated coconut. Add the soaked dal and cook covered, on low heat, till the *dal* is soft and the *bhaaji* is cooked. Garnish with chopped coriander and serve.

Note: If the seasoning is made with ghee and cumin seeds and the *dal* is substituted with peanut powder, this *bhaaji* can be eaten during a fast.

Vegetables like *doodhi* (bottle gourd), *bhopla* (pumpkin), *karli* (bitter gourd), and *vaangi* (brinjal) seem to have a common characteristic — most people hate them. While I am no great fan of the brinjal, surprisingly, whenever I am asked to come up with a vegetable for a special meal, I almost always think of *bharli vaangi*. And when you serve them as 'Stuffed Aubergines with a Tangy Coconut Sauce', they can pass off as haute cuisine! In fact, I feel that these vegetables appeal to a more discerning palate, one that has seen and tasted it all. Particularly after years of overseas living where one's palate may be deadened by synthetic tasting vegetables and bland European cooking, one can actually relish the strong taste of this purple egg-shaped vegetable. And when the person begins to pine for it, then you truly know that he has returned home after a long time away.

Karli

SPICED BITTER GOURD

Ingredients

250 g bitter gourd (*karli*), seeded and finely sliced

Salt to taste

¼ teaspoon sugar

½ teaspoon lime juice

2 tablespoons grated fresh coconut

Seasoning

1 teaspoon oil

¼ teaspoon mustard seeds

¼ teaspoon turmeric powder

¼ teaspoon red chilli powder

A pinch of asafoetida (*hing*)

Method

- Sprinkle the sliced bitter gourd with salt. Wrap in a piece of cloth and place under a weight for at least 30 minutes, so that all the bitterness drains out.
- For the seasoning, heat the oil in a pan and add the mustard seeds. When they start to splutter, add the turmeric powder, chilli powder and asafoetida. Add the bitter gourd and salt and cook on low heat, stirring occasionally, till slightly crisp. Add sugar and lime juice and garnish with grated coconut.
- Serve hot with Poli (page 130).

Bharli Vaangi

STUFFED BRINJALS

Ingredients

¼ kg brinjals (see note)
1 teaspoon freshly grated coconut
1 teaspoon chopped coriander

Stuffing

2 tablespoons gram flour
½ cup freshly grated coconut
1 tablespoon Goda Masala (page 24, 25)
2 tablespoons roasted peanut powder
2 teaspoons sugar or jaggery
Salt to taste
2 tablespoons tamarind pulp

Seasoning

1 teaspoon oil
½ teaspoon mustard seeds
¼ teaspoon turmeric powder
½ teaspoon red chilli powder
A pinch of asafoetida (*hing*)
2-3 curry leaves

Method

- Make 2 slits crossways on the rounded end of the brinjal for the *masala* stuffing.
- For the stuffing, mix together in a bowl, the gram flour, coconut, *goda masala*, peanut powder, jaggery, salt and tamarind pulp. Stuff the brinjals with this *masala* stuffing.
- For the seasoning, heat the oil in a pressure cooker or a wide thick-bottomed pan. Add the mustard seeds and when they start to splutter, add turmeric powder, chilli powder, asafoetida and curry leaves.
- Add the brinjals, ½ cup of water and cook until the pressure is released 4 times (4 whistles). If cooking in a pan, cover and simmer, with a little water on the lid. Cook till the water evaporates and the brinjals are tender and soft. Insert the point of knife into the brinjals to check if they are done.
- Serve hot, garnished with the chopped coriander and grated coconut.

Note: To make really good *bharli vaangi* look out for the plump striped brinjals with thorny stalks. The small round ones will also do.

Bharli Karli

STUFFED BITTER GOURD

While *karli* with their tiny green ridges and thin long stems look like cute tiny thorny green mice ready to scurry off, they are my least favourite *bhaaji*. I must confess though, I may be unfair for, if they are cooked well, particularly to a crisp, they can be quite interesting, their bitterness being the perfect foil to our otherwise sweetish food. And when stuffed with coconut, spice and *besan*, they do become that much harder to resist.

Ingredients

500 g baby bitter gourd (*karli*)
Salt to taste
3 tablespoons oil

Stuffing

1 teaspoon oil
1 cup gram flour
½ teaspoon red chilli powder
Salt to taste
¼ teaspoon sugar
A squeeze of lime juice
1½ teaspoons cumin powder
1½ teaspoons coriander powder
1 cup grated fresh coconut

Method

- Slit the bitter gourds lengthwise half way through, ensuring that the vegetable is still in one piece. Gently remove the seeds and hollow out the insides.
- Steep the bitter gourd in salted water.
- For the stuffing, heat 1 teaspoon oil in a pan and roast the gram flour till brown.
- Add the chilli powder, salt, sugar and a squeeze of lime, and stir. Add the cumin powder, coriander powder, and grated coconut, and sauté till fragrant.
- Stuff each gourd with the gram flour-coconut mixture and tie with a piece of string to seal the stuffing.
- Heat 3 tablespoons oil in a pressure-cooker and add the stuffed gourds, ¼ cup of water and pressure cook until the pressure is released 4 times (4 whistles), or till the gourds are soft. Alternatively, deep-fry the stuffed gourds till golden brown.

Karlyache Chaktya

SWEET AND SOUR BITTER GOURD

This dish can be a welcome change from the regular cauliflower-potato fare normally dished out in most homes.

Ingredients

500 g bitter gourd (*karli*), seeded and thinly sliced
Salt to taste
1 tablespoon tamarind
2 tablespoons jaggery
½ teaspoon red chilli powder
½ cup sesame seeds, roasted and powdered
½ cup roasted peanut powder
1 teaspoon Goda Masala (page 24, 25)
½ cup grated dried coconut

Seasoning

1 teaspoon oil
¼ teaspoon mustard seeds
¼ teaspoon turmeric powder
¼ teaspoon red chilli powder
A pinch of asafoetida (*hing*)

Method

- Sprinkle the sliced bitter gourd with salt. Wrap in a piece of cloth and place under a weight for at least 30 minutes, so that all the bitterness drains out.
- Soak the tamarind in ¼ cup of water. Squeeze out the pulp. Mix in the jaggery, chilli powder, sesame powder, peanut powder, *goda masala* and grated coconut.
- For the seasoning, heat the oil in a *kadai* and add the mustard seeds. When they start to splutter, add turmeric powder, chilli powder and asafoetida. Add the tamarind-coconut mixture and mix well.
- Add the bitter gourd and ¼ cup of water to cover the vegetable. Cook, stirring occasionally, till the vegetable is crisp.
- Serve hot with Poli (page 130).

Kartolichi Bhaaji

SPICED SPINY BITTER GOURD

The tiny spiny bitter gourd is the country cousin of the bitter gourd and not half as bitter. It grows wild during the rainy season, and I was first introduced to it as late as two years ago, when Kadam, our farm supervisor, brought home a whole heap of them from the farm. Since then, they have become a staple monsoon *bhaaji* in our home especially as they are 'organically home grown!'

Ingredients

500 g spiny bitter gourd (*kartoli*), finely sliced

Salt to taste

¼ teaspoon sugar

Stuffing

1 teaspoon oil

¼ teaspoon mustard seeds

¼ teaspoon turmeric powder

¼ teaspoon red chilli powder

A pinch of asafoetida (*hing*)

Method

- Wash the sliced gourd and drain in a colander.
- For the seasoning, heat the oil in a pan and add the mustard seeds. When they begin to splutter, add turmeric powder, chilli powder, and asafoetida.
- Add the sliced gourd and salt, and cook on low heat, stirring occasionally.
- Add the sugar to counteract the bitter taste, and continue to cook till the *bhaaji* is slightly crisp.
- Serve hot with Poli (page 130).

Kaandyachi Bhaaji

SPICED SPRING ONIONS

The strange as it may sound, onions make a tasty *bhaaji* especially if they are green spring onions.

Ingredients

1 bunch (250 g) spring onions or 250 g onions, finely sliced
2 tablespoons gram flour
Salt to taste

Seasoning

1 teaspoon oil
½ teaspoon mustard seeds
¼ teaspoon turmeric powder
¼ teaspoon red chilli powder
A pinch of asafoetida (*hing*)

Method

- Wash the green leaves of the spring onion, and chop. Slice the white bulb lengthwise.
- For the seasoning, heat the oil in a pan and add the mustard seeds. When they start to splutter, add the turmeric powder, chilli powder and asafoetida.
- Add the chopped spring onion white bulbs and cook for a few minutes.
- Add the chopped greens, cover and cook on a low heat till the *bhaaji* releases water.
- Add the gram flour and salt and cook on high heat, stirring continuously to prevent the gram flour from clumping. Cook till the gram flour no longer tastes raw.
- Serve with Poli (page 130).

Note: This *bhaaji* is specially made on *Kaande Navmi*.

Doodhichi Bhaaji

SPICED BOTTLE GOURD

This long green gourd is enjoying great popularity of late thanks to all the dieticians who can't stop singing its praises: low in fat and cholesterol, high in dietary fibre, rich in iron and Vitamins C and B complex. Its sodium and potassium content makes it suitable for hypertensive patients, for light, low-cal diets, as well as for small children, people with digestive problems, diabetics and convalescents. I am not too sure about these claims, but I can vouch for it being light to digest and easy on the stomach. I particularly like eating this *bhaaji* in the rainy season.

Ingredients

250 g bottle gourd, peeled and chopped into bite-sized pieces

5-6 cashew nuts, soaked

½ cup coconut milk

Salt to taste

A pinch of sugar or a small piece of jaggery

1 teaspoon grated coconut

1 teaspoon chopped coriander

Seasoning

1 teaspoon ghee (*toop*)

¼ teaspoon mustard seeds

½ teaspoon cumin seeds

2-3 curry leaves

½ teaspoon turmeric powder (optional)

A pinch of asafoetida (*hing*)

1 green chilli, finely chopped (optional)

Method

- For the seasoning, heat the ghee and add the mustard seeds. When they start to splutter, add the cumin seeds, curry leaves, turmeric powder, asafoetida and green chilli, if you really want it fiery hot.
- Add the bottle gourd and cashew nuts, and stir.
- Add the coconut milk, salt and cook, covered, till bottle gourd is translucent, soft, and pulpy. Add sugar and stir to mix.
- Garnish with grated coconut and chopped coriander and serve.

Note: Coconut milk can be substituted with plain milk or water.

Bhoplyachi Bhaaji

SPICED PUMPKIN

I just can't bring myself to eat the pumpkin or *bhopla* in any form. But during the monsoons, or even in summer, when vegetables are hard to come by, it can be made into a very tasty *bhaaji*. Besides, its soft texture makes it easy to cook and with an extra bit of oil, and some masala it is a healthier option than just potato and more potato.

Ingredients

250 g pumpkin, peeled and cut into bite-sized pieces

A pinch of sugar or a small piece of jaggery

1 teaspoon grated coconut

1 teaspoon chopped coriander

Salt to taste

Seasoning

1 teaspoon oil

¼ teaspoon mustard seeds

A pinch of asafoetida (*hing*)

2-3 curry leaves

½ teaspoon red chilli powder

½ teaspoon turmeric powder

1 green chilli, finely chopped (optional)

Method

- For the seasoning, heat the oil in a pan, and add the mustard seeds. When they start to splutter, add the asafoetida, curry leaves, chilli powder, turmeric powder and green chilli.
- Add the pumpkin, salt and cook, covered till soft, translucent and pulpy.
- Add sugar and stir to mix.
- Garnish with grated coconut and chopped coriander and serve.

Note: This *bhaaji* if made with a simple seasoning of ghee and cumin seeds, can be served during a fast.

THOSE LEAFY GREENS THAT MAKE YOU STRONG

According to my children, we *Kokanasthas* are obsessed with weird vegetables, which by their definition, is anything that is green and gooey and doesn't resemble a carrot, potato, cauliflower or cabbage, or what is known in our vegetable markets as 'English vegetables'. They just don't understand that a narrow coastal belt is hardly conducive to growing exotic vegetables, and since leafy greens and meandering vines bearing pumpkins and gourds grew so well around our ancestral homes, these vegetables were bound to be part of our traditional food. It is only now, with great emphasis being put on healthy diets and roughage, that these vegetables are finding favour at our tables. *Kokanasthas* on the other hand, have always included at least one leafy green or other 'weird' vegetable in their daily menu.

Paale Bhaaji

SPICED GREENS

Fenugreek (*methi*), wild spinach (*chakvat*), colocasia (*alu*), and amaranth (*math*), Malabar spinach (*maayalu*), dill (*shepu*) are very popular, but just as tasty as the brilliant red amaranthus (*laal math*). Of course, one has to make sure that they are thoroughly cleaned before cooking, and it is for this reason that they are best avoided during the rainy season.

Ingredients

1 bunch (about 200 g) any leafy vegetable

½ cup finely chopped onion

Salt to taste

A pinch of sugar

Seasoning

1 teaspoon oil

¼ teaspoon mustard seeds

¼ teaspoon turmeric powder

A pinch of asafoetida (*hing*)

1 green chilli, finely chopped

Method

- Wash the chopped greens well.
- For the seasoning, heat the oil in a pan, and add the mustard seeds. When they start to splutter, add turmeric powder, asafoetida and green chilli. Add onions and cook till soft. Add the greens and salt, and cook, covered, on low heat until soft. Add a pinch of sugar if desired.

Methichi Bhaaji

SPICED FENUGREEK

The strong bitter taste of *methi* is complemented with garlic and tempered with gram flour (*besan*). Ideally, this *bhaaji* is eaten with *bhaakri* and is lip smackingly tasty with a special garnish of hot oil and garlic poured generously on top.

Ingredients

1 tablespoon oil
½ teaspoon mustard seeds
¼ teaspoon turmeric powder
1 whole dried red chilli
2 garlic cloves, crushed
200 g finely chopped fenugreek leaves
2-3 tablespoons gram flour
1 teaspoon sugar or a small piece of jaggery

Seasoning

1 teaspoon oil
¼ teaspoon mustard seeds
¼ teaspoon turmeric powder
2 garlic cloves, crushed

Method

- Heat the oil in a *kadai* and add mustard seeds, turmeric powder, dried chilli and crushed garlic. Add the chopped fenugreek; stir well. Lower heat, cover and cook till the vegetable sweats.
- Allow most of the water to dry up and then sprinkle the gram flour and give it a good stir. Lower the heat and cook, stirring continuously, to prevent the *bhaaji* from sticking to the bottom of the pan or scorching.
- Add sugar or jaggery to counteract the bitterness of the fenugreek.
- Before serving, heat oil for seasoning in a pan and add mustard seeds, turmeric powder and garlic and take off the heat.
- The seasoning can be served on the side for each person to add according to taste, or poured on the cooked vegetable just before serving.

Note: This *bhaaji* can be made dry, by adding just enough gram flour to absorb the water that is released while cooking, or it can be soupier like a *pithla*. The other leafy green that can be made this way is dill (*shepu*). Some people also make this *bhaaji* without the *besan*, preferring to add the garlic to the seasoning at the start instead.

Paalakchi Patal Bhaaji

SPINACH WITH PEANUTS IN A BUTTERMILK GRAVY

Spinach is my favourite leafy green and I can literally make a meal of it when cooked this way. One of my friends audaciously served this dish as Spinach and Peanut Soup at an American campus restaurant specialising in ethnic organic food, way back, in the days of Woodstock and the Beatles. My father though, who is a purist in his approach to food discredits this dish as a mere impostor. According to him, the real McCoy is actually wild spinach (*chakvat*), a leafy green that is hard to come by these days, and insists that spinach is only a poor substitute. Well, whether you make it of spinach or *chakvat*, this dish is simply divine.

Ingredients

A handful of peanuts
1 tablespoon split Bengal gram
200 g spinach or wild spinach (*chakvat*), finely chopped
1 cup buttermilk
1 teaspoon gram flour
A small piece of jaggery or a pinch of sugar

Seasoning

1 teaspoon ghee (*toop*)
½ teaspoon cumin seeds
1 dried red chilli
1 inch ginger, finely chopped
3-4 garlic cloves (optional)

Method

- Soak the peanuts and the split gram for 20 minutes.
- Pressure-cook the spinach for 5 minutes till the pressure is released 2-3 times (2-3 whistles). Coarsely mash the cooked spinach and stir in the buttermilk and gram flour.
- For the seasoning, heat ghee in a *kadai* and add the cumin seeds, dried chilli and the chopped ginger and garlic. Lower the heat and add the spinach-buttermilk mixture, and bring to the boil, stirring occasionally, till the gram flour is cooked.
- Add the soaked peanuts and split gram to the spinach-buttermilk mixture, and cook for 2-3 minutes or till the gramflour is cooked. Add jaggery or a pinch of sugar for that special taste. Serve hot, with freshly cooked Bhaat (page 35).

Note: Use the slightly sour buttermilk leftover from making *toop*.

Ambaadichi Bhaaji

SPICED SORREL

This *bhaaji* is my mother-in-law's favourite and is served quite often at home especially during the rainy season when these greens grow in abundance. It has a peculiar sour taste, which not many people can appreciate at first, but believe me it can be quite addictive.

Ingredients

200 g finely chopped sorrel leaves (*ambaadi bhaaji*)

2-3 tablespoons split Bengal gram

A handful of rice

Jaggery to taste

1 teaspoon gram flour

Seasoning

1 teaspoon oil

½ teaspoon mustard seeds

A pinch of asafoetida (*hing*)

¼ teaspoon turmeric powder

3 garlic cloves

1 dried red chilli

Method

- Place the chopped sorrel, split gram, and rice in a pressure cooker, and add enough water to cover the ingredients. Pressure cook until the pressure is released 6-7 times (6-7 whistles).
- Allow the pressure to drop by itself, or if in a hurry, place the cooker under running cold water.
- Remove the lid and drain the cooked sorrel in a colander. This removes the extra sourness of the vegetable.
- For the seasoning, heat the oil in a pan and add the mustard seeds. When they start to splutter, add asafoetida, turmeric powder, garlic cloves, and dried chilli.
- Add the sorrel, jaggery and gram flour and mix together.
- Cook on low heat till the gram flour is cooked.
- Serve hot with Poli (page 130) or Bhaat (page 35).

Note: This *bhaaji* is served with a side of seasoning as used in Methichi Bhaaji (page 88).

Usal

GRAVIED LEGUMES

In today's new age nutrition, bean sprouts have suddenly gained popularity as a 'living food' particularly low in fat, and high in fibre and protein.

Usal or legumes are a staple of the *Kokanastha* diet and dried beans are particularly handy as they can be eaten all year long. In the hot summer months when vegetables are hard to come by, they are even more welcome. The beans are quick and easy to make, and can be made more flavoursome with the simplest of *phodni* or seasonings.

While they are best eaten fresh, they can also be soaked and sprouted, thereby ensuring they retain their nutritive quality. Commonly sprouted beans are moth beans (*matki*), green gram (*moong*), red lentils (*masoor*), *Bengal gram* (*chana*) and the uniquely *Kokanastha birdya* or *dalimbya* (field beans).

SPROUTING BEANS

Sprouting of beans depends on the weather. On a normal summer day, when the temperature hovers upwards of 30°C, the beans sprout almost overnight! The dried beans should be soaked overnight, or for 8-10 hours, giving them sufficient time to absorb water and become turgid. The water should be drained and the beans wrapped tight in a piece of muslin, cheese cloth, or kitchen napkin, or better still placed in a bean sprouter. Within a day, the tiny shoots emerge and the beans are ready to be used for *usal*. Of course, during the cooler seasons sprouting takes a little bit longer.

Matkichi Usal

SPICED SPROUTED MOTH BEANS

Ingredients

1 cup sprouted moth beans (*matki*)
Salt to taste
1 teaspoon grated coconut
1 teaspoon chopped coriander
1-2 *kokum* rinds
A pinch of sugar
A dash of lime juice

Seasoning

1 teaspoon oil
¼ teaspoon mustard seeds
A pinch of asafoetida (*hing*)
2-3 curry leaves
½ teaspoon red chilli powder
¼ teaspoon turmeric powder

Method

- For the seasoning, heat the oil in a pan and add the mustard seeds. When they start to splutter, add the asafoetida, curry leaves, chilli powder and turmeric powder.
- Add the moth beans and give them a good stir.
- Pour in a little water and add the salt, coconut, coriander and kokum rinds.
- Cook, covered on low heat, for 5 minutes.
- Add a pinch of sugar and a dash of lime juice.
- Serve hot with Poli (page 130) or Dahi Bhaat (page 46).

Note: This basic recipe for Usal can be used for all sprouts like red or green gram (*harbara*), fresh green peas, black-eyed beans (*chawli*), and red lentils (*masoor*). *Matkichi usal* is used to make *misal*, a popular Maharashtrian snack.

Birdyachi (Dalimbya) Usal

SPICED SPROUTED FIELD BEANS

While the recipe is similar to that of *matki*, I have made special reference to it because it is particularly enjoyed by *Kokanasthas* and is considered a delicacy. Perhaps this is because one has to spend hours skinning the plump beans! If the sprouted beans are soaked in warm water for about an hour or so, the skins come off easily when pressed and the beans just pop out! These beans are harvested in May and that is when they are available in the market.

Ingredients

1 cup sprouted field beans (*birdya/dalimbya*)
Salt to taste
1 teaspoon grated coconut
1 teaspoon chopped coriander
1-2 *kokum* rinds
A pinch of sugar
A dash of lime juice

Seasoning

1 teaspoon oil
¼ teaspoon mustard seeds
A pinch of asafoetida (*hing*)
2-3 curry leaves
½ teaspoon red chilli powder
¼ teaspoon turmeric powder
1-2 green chillies, chopped (optional)

Method

- For the seasoning, heat the oil in a pan and add the mustard seeds. When they start to splutter add asafoetida, curry leaves, chilli powder and turmeric powder.
- Add the beans and give them a good stir. Pour in a little water and add salt, coconut, coriander and *kokum* rinds. Cover and simmer for 5 minutes.
- Add a pinch of sugar and a dash of lime juice.
- Serve hot with Poli (page 130).

Mugache Kalan

SPICED SPROUTED GREEN GRAM

Ingredients

1 cup sprouted green gram (*moong*)
½ onion, finely chopped
Salt to taste
1 teaspoon grated coconut
1 teaspoon chopped coriander
1-2 *kokum* rinds
A pinch of sugar
A dash of lime juice

Seasoning

1 teaspoon oil
¼ teaspoon mustard seeds
A pinch of asafoetida (*hing*)
2-3 curry leaves
½ teaspoon red chilli powder
¼ teaspoon turmeric powder

Method

- For the seasoning, heat the oil in a pan and add the mustard seeds. When they start to splutter, add asafoetida, curry leaves, chilli powder and turmeric powder. Add the onion and fry till soft.
- Add the gram and stir well to mix. Pour in a little water and add salt, coconut, coriander and *kokum* rinds. Cover and simmer for 5 minutes.
- Add a pinch of sugar and a dash of lime.

Masoorchi Usal

SPICED SPROUTED RED LENTILS

These tiny flat salmon-coloured beans make the tastiest side dish, and if enhanced with tomato, garlic and ginger, they make a curry to give any non-vegetarian dish a run for its money. However, this is the traditional recipe.

Ingredients

½ onion, finely chopped
1 cup sprouted red lentils (*masoor*)
Salt to taste
1 teaspoon grated coconut
1 teaspoon chopped coriander
1-2 *kokum* rinds
A pinch of sugar

Seasoning

1 teaspoon oil
½ teaspoon mustard seeds
A pinch of asafoetida (*hing*)
2-3 curry leaves
½ teaspoon red chilli powder
½ teaspoon turmeric powder
1-2 green chillies, chopped (optional)

Method

- For the seasoning, heat the oil in a pan and add the mustard seeds. When they start to splutter, add asafoetida, curry leaves, chilli powder and turmeric powder. Add the onion and fry till soft.
- Add the sprouted lentils and give them a good stir. Pour in a little water and add salt, coconut, coriander and *kokum* rinds. Cover and simmer for 5 minutes.
- Add a pinch of sugar.

Note: If you substitute the water for cooking with a cup of freshly extracted coconut milk, you will get the most amazing curry!

Kansachi Usal

SPICED CORN

Unlike other *usal* this one is actually made out of fresh corn and is perfect on a monsoon day or in the winter when new corn is available in the market.

Ingredients

250 g grated fresh corn
Salt to taste
1 teaspoon chopped coriander
1 teaspoon grated coconut

Seasoning

1 teaspoon oil
¼ teaspoon mustard seeds
A pinch of asafoetida (*hing*)
2-3 curry leaves
½ teaspoon red chilli powder
½ teaspoon turmeric powder
1-2 green chillies, chopped (optional)

Method

- For the seasoning, heat the oil in a pan, add the mustard seeds. When they begin to splutter add asafoetida, curry leaves, chilli powder, turmeric powder and green chillies, if you really want it fiery hot.
- Add the grated corn and stir well. Pour in some water, lower heat, cover and allow to simmer for 5 minutes, checking from time to time.
- When the corn is done, add salt, chopped coriander and grated coconut, and serve.

Note: For a variation, add 1 finely chopped small onion to the seasoning. When the onions turn pink add the grated corn and cook with ½ cup milk instead of water.

Watanyachi Usal

SPICED GREEN PEAS

Fresh green peas are a treat and a great favourite with me and my older daughter. The peas from Mahabaleshwar are tiny and sweet, but any green peas can be used to make this mouth-watering *usal*.

Ingredients

250 g shelled fresh green peas

Salt to taste

¼ teaspoon sugar

1 teaspoon grated coconut

1 teaspoon chopped coriander

A squeeze of lime juice

Seasoning

1 teaspoon oil

¼ teaspoon mustard seeds

A pinch of asafoetida (*hing*)

2-3 curry leaves

½ teaspoon red chilli powder

¼ teaspoon turmeric powder

Method

- For the seasoning, heat the oil in a pan, add the mustard seeds. When they begin to splutter add asafoetida, curry leaves, chilli powder, and turmeric powder.
- Add the peas and stir well, adding salt and a little water, and cook on low heat. Add sugar.
- Cook till the peas are soft, and garnish with grated coconut and chopped coriander.
- I like to add a squeeze of lime to this *usal* to give it that extra tang.

Note: You can omit the turmeric powder to retain the vibrant green colour of the peas.

Interesting Asides

Chutney, Koshimbir, ani Bhareet

CHUTNEYS, SALADS AND RELISHES

Unlike other cuisines, which are served course by course or as plated meals, Indian cuisine always has an array of side dishes to choose from. These interesting asides specially cater to the sour and bitter-sweet tastes making for an attractive change between munches and also provide the nourishment that only raw food can provide. As I can't help mentioning time and again, our ancestors knew the importance of raw food and no meal was ever complete without some koshimbir or *pachadi*, pickle or chutney.

Hirvi Chutney

BASIC GREEN CHUTNEY

A must *de la cuisine*, this chutney is a godsend for the hungry person foraging in the kitchen for a quick bite, and should always be in one's refrigerator. Mixed with a generous amount of butter, this chutney makes a tasty sandwich spread which when teamed with thinly sliced cucumber and cheese makes a divine sandwich. It is also a spicy accompaniment to the otherwise bland Varan Bhaat (page 34, 35) or Poli (page 130). Needless to say, this chutney is an essential component in everyday as well as special meals.

Ingredients

2 cups freshly grated coconut
1 cup fresh coriander
2-3 green chillies, or to taste
½ teaspoon cumin seeds
1-2 cloves garlic (optional)
Juice of 1 lime
Salt to taste
Sugar to taste

Method

- In a blender, mix together all the ingredients and grind to a fine paste. You could add a little water while grinding, but make sure not to add too much.
- Refrigerate to store for a few days.

Note: This chutney can also be added to certain *usal* like *masoor* and *moong*, or even to bean or green pea *bhaaji* for added flavour.

Shengdanychi Chutney

PEANUT CHUTNEY

Ingredients

2 cups shelled peanuts
1 teaspoon cumin seeds
4 garlic cloves
1 tablespoon red chilli powder
Sugar to taste
Salt to taste

Method

- Lightly roast the peanuts in a *kadai*.
- Cool and remove the skin.
- Pound coarsely in a *khal-batta* (mortar and pestle) along with cumin seeds, garlic, chilli powder, sugar and salt.
- Some amount of oil will be released from peanuts, which makes the chutney a nice homogenous mix.

Note: This is one recipe where the mixer/blender should be avoided as the chutney can quickly turn into a spicy peanut butter instead of a coarsely ground chutney!

Mirchicha Thecha

SPICY GREEN CHILLI CHUTNEY

A hot favourite with my husband and his family, this *thecha* was actually his grandmother's staple food. I once ventured to taste this dish and cried through the rest of the meal while the rest of the family looked on in amusement. However, it didn't seem to do any harm to the rest of the family, especially his grandmother who was a strict vegetarian, had never tasted even garlic and ginger, and who lived well into her nineties. Apart from her food aphorisms (she told me that a woman should avoid eating dinner if she wanted to maintain her slim, girlish figure), she was known for her disciplined lifestyle and carried her own *thecha* whenever she visited, because she didn't trust anyone's recipe but her own. I actually got this recipe from my husband's aunt who was entrusted with the closely guarded original recipe. So here's the genuine *Akkaji's thecha*.

Ingredients

250 g green chillies, washed and wiped dry

200 g fresh coriander

½ teaspoon powdered mustard seeds

Juice of 2 limes

½ teaspoon roasted and powdered fenugreek seeds (*methi dana*)

Salt to taste

Sugar to taste

Seasoning

½ cup oil

1 teaspoon mustard seeds

Method

- Grind the green chillies and coriander to a coarse paste.
- Add the mustard and fenugreek powders, salt, sugar and lime juice and stir well.
- Heat oil in a pan and add the mustard seeds; when they splutter, pour into the *thecha*. Stir well and adjust the seasoning.

Note: To prevent the *thecha* from becoming a smooth paste, and if you can brave the pungent fumes, pound it in a mortar and pestle (*khal-batta*). This chutney keeps for about 1 month.

Tomatochi Chutney

TOMATO CHUTNEY

Ingredients

¼ cup oil
A pinch of asafoetida (*hing*)
½ kg tomatoes, chopped into small pieces
5-6 green chillies, finely chopped
Salt to taste
1 tablespoon jaggery
½ cup roasted peanut powder
1 teaspoon finely chopped coriander

Method

- Heat the oil in a pan, and add the asafoetida.
- Add the tomatoes and stir, lower heat and cook till soft and pulpy. Turn off the heat and allow to cool.
- Add the chillies, salt, jaggery, peanut powder and chopped coriander.
- Mix thoroughly and serve with hot Bhaakri (page 133) or Bhaat (page 35).

Hirvya Tomatochi Chutney

GREEN TOMATO CHUTNEY

Ingredients

½ kg green tomatoes
5-6 green chillies
½ cup freshly grated coconut
½ cup roasted peanut powder
5-6 garlic cloves
1 teaspoon coriander leaves
1 tablespoon jaggery

Method

- Chop the tomatoes and chillies into small pieces.
- Add all the ingredients in a blender jar and blend into a fine paste.

Note: If desired, top with a freshly made seasoning of oil, mustard seeds and turmeric powder.

Khamang Kakdichi Koshimbir

TANGY CUCUMBER AND PEANUT SALAD

This is my favourite salad, which usually draws 'oohs!' and 'aahs!' of appreciation from all my guests. Its crunchy peanut texture and fresh lemony flavour are hits with non-Maharashtrians as well.

Ingredients

1-2 cucumbers

2 tablespoons roasted peanut powder

1 tablespoon finely chopped green chilli (optional)

2 tablespoons freshly grated coconut

Juice of ½ lime

Salt to taste

A pinch of sugar

1 tablespoon chopped coriander

Seasoning

1 teaspoon oil

¼ teaspoon mustard seeds

2-3 curry leaves

Method

- Peel and finely dice the cucumber.
- Add the peanut powder, chopped chillies, grated coconut, lime juice, salt, sugar and coriander. Mix well.
- For the seasoning, heat the oil in *kadai* and add the mustard seeds. When they begin to splutter add the curry leaves and take off heat, and mix it into the salad and serve.
- This salad tastes best when chilled.

Variation: Use grated carrot instead of cucumber, or a mix of both for yet another variation.

Note: The specialty of this salad is that the cucumber is diced so minutely, that it is almost minced, but not grated. If eaten during *upvas* substitute the oil with ghee and the mustard seeds with cumin seeds.

Kobichi Koshimbir

TANGY CABBAGE SALAD

This is another popular salad that combines the crispness of raw cabbage with tangy lime juice.

Ingredients

½ cabbage, finely sliced
Juice of ½ lime
1 teaspoon soaked split green gram (*moong dal*)
1 teaspoon grated coconut
1 teaspoon chopped coriander
1 green chilli, finely chopped
Salt to taste
Sugar to taste

Seasoning

1 teaspoon oil
¼ teaspoon mustard seeds
2-3 curry leaves

Method

- In a bowl, mix all the ingredients together.
- For the seasoning, heat the oil in *kadai* and add the mustard seeds. When they begin to splutter add the curry leaves and take off heat, and mix it into the salad.

Tomato-Kaanda Koshimbir

TOMATO AND ONION SALAD

My mother-in-law tells me that this childhood favourite was called *tanto* in her maternal home, while my mother calls it a very ordinary standby, and an apology for a *koshimbir*. However, when there is no other salad available, this is a quick and tasty side dish that complements most food.

Ingredients

2 ripe tomatoes, finely chopped

1 medium onion, finely chopped

2 tablespoons coarsely powdered roasted peanuts

2 tablespoons freshly grated coconut

1 green chilli, finely sliced

1 teaspoon chopped coriander

Seasoning

1 teaspoon oil

¼ teaspoon mustard seeds

2-3 curry leaves

Method

- Mix together all the ingredients.
- For the seasoning, heat the oil in *kadai* and add the mustard seeds. When they begin to splutter add the curry leaves and take off heat, and mix it into the salad and serve.

Beetchi Koshimbir

BEETROOT SALAD

This delightful pink salad is very popular and can be made either with the seasoning or without. In which case, the extra zing is added by powdered mustard seeds.

Ingredients

1 beetroot

½ cup yoghurt

1-2 green chillies, finely chopped

1 tablespoon finely chopped coriander

½ teaspoon powdered mustard seeds (optional)

Seasoning

1 tablespoons ghee (*toop*)

½ teaspoon mustard or cumin seeds

Method

- Steam the beetroot in a pressure cooker. Cool, peel and grate or chop it finely.
- Beat the yoghurt until smooth.
- Mix together in a bowl, the beetroot, chopped chillies, coriander and powdered mustard seeds. Pour in the yoghurt and mix well.
- For the seasoning, heat ghee in a pan and add cumin seeds and take off the heat.
- Stir the seasoning into the salad.

Vaangyache Bhareet

SMOKED BRINJAL RELISH

The distinctive smoky flavour of the *bhareet* truly lifts up any meal.

Ingredients

1 large firm brinjal
1 onion, finely chopped
1 green chilli, finely chopped
1 tablespoon chopped fresh coriander
Salt to taste

Seasoning

2 teaspoons oil
1 teaspoon mustard seeds
¼ teaspoon turmeric powder
A pinch of asafoetida (*hing*)
2-3 curry leaves

Method

- Roast the brinjal over an open flame turning it from time to time to ensure that it is roasted evenly.
- When the skin is charred, take off the flame and set aside to cool.
- Peel the burnt skin off and mash the brinjal to a pulp.
- For the seasoning, heat the oil in a pan, and add the mustard seeds. When they start to splutter, add turmeric powder, asafoetida and curry leaves.
- Add the chopped onion, mashed brinjal, chilli, coriander, and salt and cook till the brinjal is soft.

Variation: To make *Kolache bhareet* (brinjal and coconut milk relish), just add coconut milk to taste.

Bhoplyache Bhareet

PUMPKIN RELISH

Ingredients

2 cups diced pumpkin
Salt to taste

½ cup yoghurt, whisked or
½ cup coconut milk + 1 teaspoon tamarind pulp

Seasoning

1 tablespoon oil
¼ teaspoon mustard seeds

¼ teaspoon turmeric powder
A pinch of asafoetida (*hing*)

Method

- Steam the pumpkin for 2 minutes.
- Mash and add salt to taste. Mix with whipped yoghurt.
- Alternatively, add tamarind pulp to the pumpkin along with the coconut milk.
- For the seasoning, heat the oil in a pan and add the mustard seeds. When they start to splutter add turmeric powder and asafoetida and take off the heat.
- Pour seasoning over the pumpkin mixture, stir and serve.

Note: If eaten during *upvas* substitute the oil with ghee (*toop*) and the mustard seeds with cumin seeds.

Kakdiche Kayras

CUCUMBER AND PEANUT RELISH

This is one recipe where you work backwards, by making the seasoning first.

Ingredients

A small lump of tamarind
½ red chilli powder
¾ cup roasted peanut powder
¼ cup powdered sesame seeds
½ cup jaggery
Salt to taste
2 cups finely chopped cucumber

Seasoning

2 teaspoons oil
1 teaspoon mustard seeds
A pinch of asafoetida (*hing*)
2-3 curry leaves
1 teaspoon Goda Masala (page 24, 25)

Method

- Soak the tamarind in ½ cup of water for 10 minutes till it softens, and squeeze out the pulp.
- For the seasoning, heat the oil in a small *kadai* and add mustard seeds. When they start to splutter add asafoetida, curry leaves, and *goda masala* and fry for a few seconds.
- Then add the tamarind pulp, chilli powder, peanut powder, powdered sesame seeds, jaggery and salt to taste. Stir and bring to a boil.
- Cool and add the mixture to the chopped cucumber, mix well and serve.

Note: *Kayras* is essentially a sweet and sour salad that is eaten in small quantities and serves as a palate teaser.

Peruche Kayras

GUAVA RELISH

Ingredients

A small lump of tamarind
½ teaspoon red chilli powder
1 tablespoon roasted peanut powder
½ cup jaggery
Salt to taste
1 cup peeled and finely chopped guava

Seasoning

2 teaspoons oil
1 teaspoon mustard seeds
¼ teaspoon fenugreek seeds
2-3 curry leaves
1 teaspoon Goda Masala (page 24, 25)

Method

- Soak the tamarind in ½ cup of water for 10 minutes till it softens and squeeze out the pulp.
- For the seasoning, heat the oil in a small *kadai* and add mustard seeds. When they start to splutter add the fenugreek seeds, curry leaves, and *goda masala* and fry for a few seconds.
- Add the tamarind pulp, chilli powder, peanut powder, jaggery and salt to taste. Stir and bring to a boil.
- Add in the chopped guava and cook till soft.

Kairiche Kayras

GREEN MANGO RELISH

Ingredients

A small lump of tamarind

2 cups peeled and chopped unripe mango

2 cups jaggery

Salt to taste

1 teaspoon red chilli powder

Seasoning

2 teaspoons oil

1 teaspoon mustard seeds

½ teaspoon fenugreek seeds

A pinch of asafoetida (*hing*)

Method

- Soak the tamarind in ½ cup of water for 10 minutes till it softens and squeeze out the pulp.
- For the seasoning, heat the oil in a small *kadai* and add mustard seeds. When they start to splutter add fenugreek seeds, asafoetida, and fry for a few seconds.
- Add chopped mango, lower the heat, cover and cook for 2-3 minutes till the mangoes are soft.
- Add the tamarind pulp, jaggery, salt and chilli powder and cook for another 2-3 minutes.
- You can add a little water for a more liquid *kayras*.

Karvandache Kayras

BENGAL CURRANT SALAD

The *karvanda* shrub grows wild in the Konkan region and along the East coast, with fruit that looks very much like a black grape, which is why it is sometimes referred to as Bengal currant.

Ingredients

1 small lump of tamarind
1 cup Bengal currant (*karvanda*)
1 cup jaggery
½ teaspoon red chilli powder
Salt to taste

Seasoning

2 teaspoons oil
1 teaspoon mustard seeds
¼ teaspoon fenugreek seeds
2-3 curry leaves
1 teaspoon Goda Masala (page 24, 25)

Method

- Soak the tamarind in ½ cup of water for 10 minutes till it softens and squeeze out the pulp.
- Soak the *karvanda* in water to remove any sticky sap. Pat dry and pound coarsely. Set aside.
- For the seasoning, heat the oil in a *kadai*, and add the mustard seeds. When they start to splutter, add fenugreek seeds, curry leaves, and *goda masala* and fry for a few seconds.
- Add the tamarind pulp, jaggery, chilli powder, and salt and bring to the boil.
- Add the berries and cook till the fruit is soft.

Morambe, Lonchi ani Papdya

JAMS, PICKLES AND CRISPS

JOYS OF SUMMER

Summer holidays in my childhood meant mango time and endless days of playing with cousins, meeting family at weddings, and helping with the preparation of pickles and jams. Many people believe that pickles and jams are the refuge of the inept cook, because anything that is oily and spicy or sweet and sticky is bound to taste good. Having heard this at least a million times from my father, pickles were almost banned from our table by my mother who took pride in the fact that her everyday food was much appreciated by all those who ate with us and not in need of any other embellishment. Surprisingly though, she did go through the summer and winter pickle routine, making them diligently in copious quantities and distributing them to all and sundry. At the end of the day pickles and jams do add some magic to the food which can be quite humdrum on a daily basis.

Hapoosacha Moramba

ALPHONSO MANGO JAM

One particularly *Kokanastha* summer delight is mango jam or *moramba* made out of *hapoos* or Alphonso mangoes. Needless to say, this delicious preserve is eaten faster than it is made, and it is just as well, because it doesn't keep for long.

Ingredients

½ cup sugar
2 cloves
4 cardamoms, powdered
3-4 saffron threads
2-3 ripe Alphonso mangoes, peeled and diced

Method

- In a pan on medium heat, dissolve the sugar in ¼ cup of water. Cook till the syrup thickens and is slightly sticky.
- Add the cloves, powdered cardamom and saffron.
- Add the diced mango and cook on low heat till the jam thickens and gets a shiny glaze.
- Cool and store in an airtight jar.

Makes 300 grams

Moramba - I

GREEN MANGO JAM - I

This is the more traditional mango jam that all of us have grown up with, and is made in June after the first monsoon shower. To make the best *moramba* you will require the greenest and sourest Rajapuri mangoes. The mangoes can be used in two ways: either in large chunky bits or finely grated.

Ingredients

2 kg Rajapuri mangoes, peeled and diced

4 kg sugar

10 g cardamom, coarsely ground

A pinch of saffron threads

Method

- Steam the mangoes until soft. Spread out the steamed mangoes on a dry kitchen towel for 2 hours.
- Make a thick sugar syrup with the sugar and a little water, ground cardamom and saffron. Make sure the syrup does not become thicker than the consistency of honey, as it will crystallise.
- While the syrup is still warm, add the mango and cook on low heat till the mixture reaches the consistency of jam.

Makes approximately 2 kg

Moramba - II

GREEN MANGO JAM - II

This is made with grated mangoes.

Ingredients

2 kg Rajapuri mango, peeled and grated
4 kg sugar
10 g powdered cardamom
3-4 cloves
A pinch of saffron threads

Method

- Squeeze out the water from the grated mango.
- Place the grated mango in a thick-bottomed pan and add the sugar. Mix well and set aside for 2 hours.
- Place the pan on low heat and cook, stirring occasionally. Alternatively, the mango and sugar can be cooked together in a pressure cooker until the pressure is released twice or thrice (2-3 whistles).
- Add the cardamom, cloves and saffron and cook till the mixture becomes sticky.
- Set aside to cool and then transfer to an airtight jar.

Note: This *moramba* can also be made without any cooking. Transfer the mango mixture to a transparent airtight jar and place in direct sunlight for at least 15 days.

Morawla

INDIAN GOOSEBERRY JAM

The big fat Indian gooseberry or *awla* is suppose to have the highest concentration of Vitamin C. I remember coming across a jar of black goop hiding behind some jam jars in the far corner of the kitchen shelf. I was about to throw it away when my mother-in-law walked in and stopped me. "It's a 25 year old *morawla*" she said, "made with home-grown *awla*. It took me all of two hours to make and now since it is so old, it's even more medicinal!" Naturally, I looked at the dusty bottle with new found respect and put it back on the shelf reverentially. It has remained untouched ever since.

Ingredients

1 kg Indian gooseberry (*awla*)
1½ kg sugar
10 g powdered cardamom
A pinch of saffron threads

Method

- Prick the gooseberries all over with a fork; place them in a colander in a pressure cooker with a little water, and cook till the pressure is released twice (2 whistles) or steam in a perforated steamer.
- Make a sugar syrup of 2-string consistency with ½ cup of water, sugar, powdered cardamom and saffron.
- Place the steamed gooseberries in a container and add the sugar syrup and mix well. Place in the cooker over a little water and cook again till the pressure is released twice (2 whistles).
- Cool and transfer to an airtight jar.

Note: Even when cooked, *awla* can be hard to chop finely, so it is advisable to coarsely chop the steamed *awla*, or better still grate it so that the end product is easier to eat. The best time to make this jam is in the winter when this gooseberry is easily available in the market.

Ambyache Lonche - I

MANGO PICKLE - I

Once again the best mangoes for this pickle are the large Rajapuri ones. The mangoes should be firm with a smooth, fleshy pulp. Stringy mango does not a good pickle make.

Ingredients

1 kg unripe mangoes, unpeeled
100 grams salt
1 cup skinless split mustard seeds (*moharichi dal*)
½ cup red chilli powder
1 teaspoon oil
2 teaspoons fenugreek seeds
4 teaspoons asafoetida (*hing*)

Seasoning

250 ml oil
1 teaspoon mustard seeds
¼ cup turmeric powder

Method

- Dice the mangoes and sprinkle them with salt. Set aside for 30 minutes. Then add the split mustard seeds, and chilli powder and mix well.
- Heat the oil in a pan and fry the fenugreek seeds and asafoetida.
- Cool and grind to a fine powder and add to the mango mixture.
- For the seasoning, heat the oil in a pan until very hot, and take off the heat. Allow the oil to cool a bit and then add the mustard seeds. When they start to splutter, add the turmeric powder.
- Cool and add to the mango mixture.
- Transfer to a porcelain or airtight jar.

Ambyache Lonche - II

MANGO PICKLE - II

This is my mother's adaptation of the traditional recipe pandering to my father's passion for garlic.

Ingredients

1 kg unripe mangoes, unpeeled
100 grams salt
1 cup skinless split mustard seeds (*moharichi dal*), coarsely ground
1 cup red chilli powder
1 teaspoon oil
2 teaspoons fenugreek seeds
2 teaspoons asafoetida (*hing*)
200 grams garlic cloves, peeled

Seasoning

500 ml oil
2 tablespoons mustard seeds
50 grams dried red chillies, broken into bits

Method

- Dice the mangoes and sprinkle them with salt. Set aside for 30 minutes. Then add the ground split mustard seeds, and chilli powder and mix well.
- Heat the oil in a pan and fry the fenugreek seeds and asafoetida.
- Cool and grind to a fine powder and add to the mango mixture.
- Add the garlic cloves to the mixture.
- For the seasoning, heat the oil in a pan until very hot, and take off the heat.
- Allow the oil to cool a bit and then add the mustard seeds. When they start to splutter, add the dried chillies. Cool and add to the mango mixture.
- Transfer to a porcelain or airtight jar.

Limbache Lonche - I

LIME PICKLE - I

We sometimes use the words 'lemon' and 'lime' interchangeably. Lemons are usually large, oval, with thick bright yellow skins. Limes are smaller, round, can be both green and yellow, and have skins of varying thickness. Limes are what we commonly use in India, which all are similar to key limes, Mexican limes and Persian limes that are available abroad.

In order to make a good lime pickle, you should ensure that you select limes with thin skin, the thinner the skin the better. There are several ways of making this yummy pickle.

Ingredients

12 large limes
2 teaspoons oil
1 teaspoon asafoetida (*hing*)
1 teaspoon fenugreek seeds
2 teaspoons turmeric powder
½ cup red chilli powder
1½ cups salt

Method

- Quarter the limes, leaving them attached at the base.
- Heat the oil in a pan and fry the asafoetida and fenugreek seeds for a few seconds.
- Take off the heat and add turmeric powder, chilli powder and salt.
- Stuff the limes with this mixture. Sprinkle them with a little extra salt to prevent them from spoiling.
- Transfer the stuffed limes to an airtight jar and leave to stand for 15 days. Stir occasionally.
- The pickle is ready once the limes are soft.

Note: If the pickle is too salty, add some extra lime juice.

Limbache Lonche - II

LIME PICKLE - II

Ingredients

12 limes
½ cup red chilli powder
1 cup salt
½ kg sugar or jaggery

Method

- Cut each lime into 8 wedges.
- Mix together the chilli powder, salt and sugar or jaggery in a bowl.
- Add the lime wedges and mix well.
- The measure of salt and sugar is not sacrosanct – it can be adjusted to taste. Leave to mature in an airtight jar.

Note: This pickle is ready to eat in a week. If you want a deeper red hue, add a few threads of saffron. However, if you use jaggery instead of sugar, do not add saffron.

Limbache Lonche – III

LAZY LIME PICKLE

This is by far the easiest way of making a simple lime pickle, which is why I have christened it Lazy Lime Pickle !

Ingredients

12 whole limes
¼ kg salt

Method

- Place the whole limes in an airtight jar or *maath*.
- Add the salt, mix well and leave to stand in the sun for about 2 months.
- Stir well once a day so that the limes are evenly coated with the salt.
- When they get wrinkly and soft, the lime pickle is ready to eat.

Note: This pickle is medicinal and is ironically very useful in combating acidity.

Tomatoche Lonche

TOMATO PICKLE OR CHUTNEY

My husband's aunt from Kolkata was famed for her pickles and every winter she would make bottles and bottles of these chutneys from the tomatoes ripening in her garden. Tomato pickle is best made in the winter when the market is flooded with the plump red fruit.

Ingredients

10-15 garlic cloves
1 inch ginger
10-12 green chillies
3 teaspoons cumin powder
2 teaspoons red chilli powder
2 teaspoons turmeric powder
1½ cups vinegar
½ litre oil
1 kg tomatoes, quartered
Salt to taste
Sugar to taste

Method

- Finely chop half the garlic, half the ginger and green chillies and set aside.
- Grind together the remaining ginger and garlic to a fine paste.
- In a bowl, soak cumin powder, chilli powder and turmeric powder in half the vinegar for 10 minutes.
- Grind together to make a fine paste.
- Heat the oil in a pressure cooker or pressure pan, and add the ground spices. Roast till fragrant.
- Add the chopped garlic, ginger and green chillies. Sauté for about 1 minute, and add the tomatoes, salt and sugar.
- Cook, stirring, for another minute, and add the remaining vinegar. Pressure-cook till the pressure is released twice (2 whistles).
- When the oil floats on top of the tomato, it means that the pickle is done.

Mirchiche Lonche

GREEN CHILLI PICKLE

Ingredients

1 kg green chillies, cut into ½-inch pieces
250 g salt
1 cup skinless split mustard seeds
1 cup lime juice
250 ml oil
2 teaspoons fenugreek seeds
4 teaspoons asafoetida (*hing*)
2 tablespoons mustard seeds
1 tablespoon turmeric powder

Method

- Place the green chillies in a bowl; add salt, split mustard seeds, and lime juice and mix well.
- Heat a little oil in a pan and add the fenugreek seeds and asafoetida and fry for a few seconds. Remove from heat, cool and grind together to a fine powder. Set aside.
- Heat the remaining oil in a pan and add the mustard seeds. When they start to splutter, add the turmeric powder and fry for a few seconds. Remove from heat and cool. Add to the chopped chillies along with the ground fenugreek-asafoetida powder.
- Transfer to an airtight jar and leave to stand in direct sunlight for 15 days.

CRISPY DELIGHTS

Papdya (rice or sago crisps) are tiny discs made from rice or sago. Often, my mother used to add a bit of food colour to make them slightly more interesting. No special meal is complete without something crunchy to munch on. This adds a different texture to the meal.

Papad normally served is made of skinless split black gram (*uradachi dal*). Equally popular are *pohyache papad* made out of beaten rice flour and *batatyache papad* made out of potato. With space being a major constraint these days, I doubt any housewife will venture making *papad* at home.

I generally sun-dry the store brought *pohyache papad* so that they last longer. *Papad* can also be roasted on an open flame to avoid piling on the calories. I often make papdya, which are much smaller than *papad*, and can easily be sun-dried, in my small balcony.

Sabudanyachya Papdya

SAGO CRISPS

Ingredients

1 cup sago (*sabudana*)
½ teaspoon cumin seeds
Salt to taste
Oil for deep-frying

Method

- Wash and soak the sago overnight. In the morning, measure the quantity of puffed sago and take twice that quantity of water.
- Add cumin seeds and salt. Cook the mixture on medium heat, stirring continuously to make a smooth paste that coats the back of the spoon. Remove from heat.
- Place a clean sheet of plastic on a tray. Spread a tablespoonful of paste on the plastic sheet in circular motion to make a 2-inch disc. Repeat till all the paste is utilised.
- Leave to dry in the sun and store in an airtight container.
- Deep-fry in sufficient oil and serve.

Note: Poppy seeds are not used since these *papdya* are eaten during a fast.

Tandulachya Papdya

RICE CRISPS

Ingredients

1 kg rice, good quality like Ambemohar

½ teaspoon asafoetida (*hing*)

1 tablespoon poppy seeds (*khus khus*)

1 teaspoon cumin seeds

1 teaspoon salt

Oil for deep-frying

Method

- Wash the rice and leave to dry. Then grind to a fine flour.
- For 1 measure of rice flour add 3 measures of water, asafoetida, poppy seeds and cumin seeds and salt and mix.
- Cook the mixture on medium heat, stirring continuously to make a smooth paste that coats the back of the spoon. Remove from heat.
- Place a clean sheet of plastic on a tray.
- Spread a tablespoonful of paste on the plastic sheet in circular motion to make a 2-inch disc. Repeat till all the paste is utilised.
- Leave to dry in the sun and store in an airtight container.
- Deep-fry in sufficient oil and serve.

Note: Another particular favourite is the *pohyacha papad* – made out of beaten rice (*pohe*) flour.

Kurdaya – I

WHOLEWHEAT CRISPS

A popular summer past time was making papads. Even though most people buy them, the store bought ones are often left to dry out properly in the sun. Favourite crisps are *kurdaya*, *papdya* and of course *papad* made from different *dal*.

Ingredients

1 kg wheat
1 teaspoon salt
½ teaspoon asafoetida (*hing*)
Oil for deep-frying

Method

- Soak the wheat for 3 days, changing the water everyday.
- On the third day, drain the water, and grind the soaked wheat to a paste; adding more water if required.
- Essentially this is to remove the chaff. So once the wheat is ground, strain to remove the chaff.
- Leave to rest overnight. The next morning, drain the excess water that rises to the top, and measure the white wheat solid (gluten) that remains. Take an equal quantity of water and add salt and asafoetida to it.
- Boil the water on medium heat, and add the white wheat solid (gluten) stirring continuously to ensure it doesn't become lumpy.
- Cook till it becomes thick, transparent and glossy.
- Remove from the heat and allow to cool a bit.
- Press out the solid mass through a *shev* maker in a circular motion on a plastic sheet.
- Leave to dry in the sun. When dry, store in an airtight container.
- Deep-fry in sufficient oil till light and crispy. These easily turn brown so be careful while frying.
- Serve with Masaale Bhaat (page 40), Khichadi (page 36), or just eat on a rainy day!

Kurdaya – II

CRISPY CORNFLOUR SPIRALS

My mother's take on this traditional dish is given below. Exceptionally easy for the lazy cook!

Ingredients

1 cup cornflour
Salt to taste
½ teaspoon asafoetida (*hing*)
Oil for deep-frying

Method

- Mix together the cornflour and 1 cup of water and set aside.
- Add salt and asafoetida to the cornflour and cook on medium heat, stirring continously, on medium heat, until you get a thick lump.
- Press out this lump through a *shev* press on a plastic sheet into spirals.
- Leave to dry in the sun.
- Store in an air-tight container. Deep-fry in sufficient oil and serve.

Poli, Puri ani Bhaakri

ASSORTED FLATBREADS AND DEEP-FRIED PUFFED BREAD

Rice is our staple food, but what makes a *Kokanastha* meal special is the *poli* or basic wheat bread. The traditional *poli* looks easy enough to make but according to my father, *poli* are what distinguish a cook from a good cook! And perhaps he is right, because the perfect *poli* is soft, flaky and so tasty that it can be eaten plain! *Poli*-making has several nuances that are hard to explain, especially as written instructions.

Besides, at the best of times the outcome is neither universal nor standardised. There are several factors at play: the quality of wheat, the quantity of water, the amount of kneading, the way in which the *poli* is rolled out, and finally even the temperature at which it is cooked. Indeed, my sister-in-law who is a trained chef claims that only if you make thousand *poli* will you get the perfect *poli* (at least your idea of perfect). But this shouldn't discourage you from trying, as nothing ventured, nothing gained. In modern households where time is at a premium, and cutting down on fats is the norm, *poli* have been replaced by the *phulka* for everyday meals.

For special occasions, like weddings, or when *aamras* and *shrikhand* grace the menu, nothing can beat the strong robust taste of the *puri*, plump and deep-fried to perfection.

Poli

LAYERED FLATBREAD

Ingredients

3 cups wholewheat flour (*atta*)
½ teaspoon salt or to taste
1 tablespoon oil + for brushing
Ghee (*toop*), as required

Method

- Sift the flour. Add salt, 1 tablespoon oil and 1¼ cups of water, and knead to make a pliable dough. Set aside, covered, for 10 minutes, as dough rolled out instantly after kneading, yields hard, brittle *poli*.
- Divide the dough into 15 equal balls. Sprinkle a little flour over a board (*polpaat*) and roll out each ball into a 3-inch disc. Brush with a thin coat of oil and dust with a little flour.
- Fold the disc in half and brush again with oil, dusting a little flour; fold in half again to form a triangle.
- Dust the triangle with flour and roll out into a 6-inch disc.
- Heat the *tawa* and roast the *poli* on low heat. When the *poli* begins to leave the *tawa*, flip it over. Gently press the *poli* so that it cooks evenly.
- Flip it over again and allow the *poli* to rise.
- Take it off the *tawa* and smear with ghee.

Note: A good *poli* will have three flaky layers, and will be slightly browned and crisp on top. It is a common practice to make *phodnichi poli* out of leftover *poli*, for breakfast the next day, or even as a tea-time snack. They are particularly popular in smaller villages. This tasty dish is made by tearing up the *poli* into tiny bits, and adding it to a seasoning of mustard seeds and turmeric powder, with peanuts and green chillies to add that extra zing. If the dough is made with milk instead of water, the *poli* are softer and stay longer. These *poli* are called *dashmi*.

Phulka

SIMPLE FLATBREAD

This seemingly easier version of *poli* still requires some practice before the perfect *phulka* rises majestically on the *tawa*. Unlike the *poli* though, it tastes best when fresh and should be eaten straight off the *tawa*.

Ingredients

3 cups wholewheat flour
½ teaspoon salt or to taste
1 tablespoon oil
Ghee (*toop*), as required

Method

- Sift the flour and make a well in the middle. Add the salt, 1 tablespoon oil and 1¼ cups of water and knead well to make a soft, pliable dough.
- Divide the dough into 30 small equal balls. Sprinkle a little flour over the board (*polpaat*) and roll out the balls into thin 6 or 7-inch discs.
- Heat a *tawa* and roast the *phulka* on one side until small bubbles start to appear on the surface, then flip it over. Lower the heat, and allow cooking on the other side.
- Lift the *phulka* off the *tawa* and place on an open flame till it puffs up, balloon like. Take off the open flame and quickly brush with ghee.

Note: Ghee (*toop*) keeps the *phulka* soft, especially if it is going to be eaten later.

Puri

DEEP-FRIED PUFFED BREAD

Like the story of The Granny and the Pumpkin, all of us have been brought up on the story of the Runaway *Puri* - where the errant *puri* was being pursued by the whole village. I remember watching the little *puri* puffing away in the hot bubbling fat with rapt attention,waiting for it to jump out and run away before my granny could lift it out of the oil. Obviously, it never did!

Ingredients

3 cups wholewheat flour
¼ teaspoon salt or to taste
1 tablespoon oil
+ for deep-frying

Method

- Sift the flour and add the salt, 1 tablespoon oil and 1 cup of water and knead well to make a pliable dough. The dough for the *puri* should be slightly firmer than that for *poli* or *phulka*.
- Divide the dough into lime-sized small balls and roll out on a slightly greased rolling board, into 4-inch discs.
- The puri should be evenly rolled out so that it puffs up completely. Heat the oil in a *kadai*, gently lower 2-3 *puri* one by one into the hot oil.
- Lower the heat and flip them over. Fry till they puff up and rise to the surface. Drain on absorbent paper.

Note: To make perfectly crisp *puri*, add 1 teaspoon fine semolina while making the dough.

Bhaakri

SORGHUM OR MILLET FLATBREADS

Flatbread made out of sorghum (*jowar*) or millet (*bajra*) is still very popular in rural households. Even though it is a healthier option than *poli* or *phulka*, it has very few takers among the younger generation. This can be attributed to the *bhaakri's* strong taste, rougher texture, and perhaps because more skill involved, as no oil is added to soften the dough. However, *bhaakri* are invaluable for their fibre content and the feeling of fullness that even half a *bhaakri* can impart. To ensure complete authenticity, roast the *bhaakri* on a cast iron *tawa* which guarantees a more robust and rustic bread. *Bhaakri* with a sprinkling of sesame seeds on top is specially served on *Bhogi*, the festival celebrated on the eve of *Sankranti*.

Ingredients

2 cups sorghum (*jowar*)
or millet (*bajra*) flour

¼ teaspoon salt or to taste

1 cup warm water

Sesame seeds (optional)

Method

- Sift the flour, add the salt, warm water and knead well to make a smooth, pliable dough.
- Divide the dough into 2 large balls and flatten each one by hand, turning it while patting it flat, into a thin disc, on a well-floured *paraat*.
- Heat the *tawa* and roast the *bhaakri* with the floured side facing upwards. Sprinkle a handful of water on the *bhaakri* and spread it evenly. Some people (especially during the winter months) like to sprinkle a few sesame seeds on the *bhaakri* at this stage.
- Cook for about a minute, flip it over and lower the heat. Remove with an *ulatna* (flat ladle) and place on on an open flame till the *bhaakri* puffs up like a *phulka*.

Note: It is a common practice to make *phodni chi bhaakri* out of leftover *bhaakri* for the following day's breakfast. This extremely tasty dish is made with pieces of stale *bhaakri* torn into bits and mixed with a seasoning of curry leaves, mustard seeds, onions and peanuts fried in oil. A first-timer will get most disheartened because the perfect *bhaakri* needs a lot of practice. If the dough is made with milk instead of water, the *bhaakri* are softer and are called *dashmi*. During summer, *jowar bhaakri* is eaten because it is lighter, while the monsoons and winter are ideal for the darker, slightly heavier *bajra bhaakri* which is more difficult to digest.

Gaakar

THICK WHOLEWHEAT FLATBREAD

My father-in-law, who is from Nagpur, often asks for this version of *poli* especially during the monsoons. Thick and brown, this small *poli* is very easy to make and has a robustness that makes it a welcome change from the regular, everyday *poli*.

Ingredients

2 cups wholewheat flour
¼ teaspoon salt or to taste
Oil for drizzling

Method

- Sift the flour, add the salt, warm water as required, and knead well to make a soft dough.
- Divide the dough into medium-sized balls and flatten into a ¼-inch thick, 2½-inch discs, deftly turning it while patting it flat with your hand, on a well-floured board (*polpaat*).
- Heat a *tawa*; place the *gaakar* on it, and make a hole in the centre. Drizzle some oil in the hole and along the sides.
- Flip it over and press down for even cooking.

Shikran Poli

FLATBREAD WITH BANANAS AND MILK

Another mouth-watering dish intended to nurture tiny little babies into 'strong and healthy' adults, is *shikran poli*. For many of us, this is a staple and I know a middle-aged cousin of my husband who insists on eating this dish every single day!

Ingredients

1 Poli (page 130)
1 banana
½ cup milk
1 teaspoon sugar

Method

- Tear up the *poli* into tiny pieces.
- Mash the banana with milk and sugar.
- Add the *poli* to the mashed banana, and spoon into the baby's mouth.

Shikran can also be eaten outside the nursery, but in a more grown up way with the *shikran* being scooped up in individual bites of *poli* rather than being downed as a goopy mess.

Puran Poli

FLATBREADS WITH SWEET GRAM FILLING

Kokanasthas seem to have a genetic predisposition to sweets and sweet food, which is why we make sweet *poli*.

Ingredients

Puran (Stuffing)

2 cups split Bengal gram (*chana dal*)
A pinch of salt
2 cups grated jaggery or sugar
6-10 saffron threads
1 tablespoon cardamom powder

Poli

½ cup wholewheat flour
½ cup refined flour
A pinch or 1 teaspoon salt
6 tablespoons oil, or as required
1 cup rice flour, for dusting

Method

- For the *puran*, wash the split gram and soak in hot water for at least 10 minutes and upto an hour. Drain.
- Add 2½ cups of water with a pinch of salt; cook in a pressure cooker till the pressure is released 10 times (10 whistles). Alternatively, cook in a pan for about 20 minutes till very soft. The *dal* should crumble when you gently press it with your fingers.
- Drain and reserve the water from the *dal* to make Katachi Aamti (page 58).
- Add jaggery, saffron threads and powdered cardamom to the drained *dal* and mix well to make the *puran*. Cook till the mixture comes together and leaves the side of the pan. Stir occasionally to prevent the mixture from sticking at the bottom. Take off the heat and mash the *puran* with a potato masher and set aside to cool.
- Place the *puran* in the *puran patra* or a food processor and process until it becomes a smooth dough. Make sure there are no lumps or grains of unmashed *dal*. As the *puran* is ground finer, it becomes lighter in colour and dry.
- Divide the *puran* into 6 equal balls. Set aside.
- For the *poli*, sift together the wholewheat and refined flours and salt. Add 2 tablespoons oil and ½ cup of water and knead to make a sticky, elastic dough (the dough should stick to your fingers while kneading).

- Add 4 tablespoons oil, knead again and leave the dough to rest for at least 1 hour. Divide the dough into 6 equal balls.
- Flatten each ball between the palms of your hands and place a portion of stuffing in the centre. Gather the edges together to seal the stuffing. Flatten into a patty.
- Dip the patty in rice flour and roll it out into thin 7-inch round chapati on a well-floured board (*polpaat*).
- Heat a *tawa*. Dust the excess flour off the *poli* with a fine cloth, and place on the tawa.
- Lower the heat and roast the *poli* flipping it just once, as too much handling will cause it to break.
- Drizzle a little ghee on the *poli* while roasting to give it a slight glaze and enhance the taste.
- Fold the *poli* in half and gently take it off the *tawa*.
- Leave to cool on absorbent paper, before storing in an airtight container.
- Warm in a microwave just before serving with generous helpings of molten ghee.

Note: It is important to knead the dough well. The oil makes the dough more pliable and produces a crisp, flaky (rather than hard/tough) consistency when cooked. Many *Kokanasthas* like to tear this *poli* into shreds, douse it in milk and pour ghee over to create that to-die-for taste.

Gool Poli

WHOLEWHEAT FLATBREADS WITH JAGGERY FILLING

Unlike *puran poli*, this bread is extremely difficult to make. It is generally made at *Makarsankranti*, in January, when the cool breezes of winter still linger in the air, making this a treat to look forward to.

Ingredients

3 cups wholewheat flour
¾ cup oil
Salt to taste
4 cups grated jaggery
½ cup gram flour
½ cup poppy seeds (*khus khus*), roasted and pound
10-15 cardamoms, peeled and powdered
1 cup rice flour

Method

- Place the wheat flour in a large round shallow metal dish (*paraat*); add ¼ cup hot oil, and salt, and knead to make a stiff dough.
- Pound the jaggery in a mortar and pestle (*khalbatta*) with 2 teaspoons oil to prevent it from sticking.
- Lightly roast the gram flour. Add the pounded jaggery, poppy seeds and powdered cardamom. Mix together and knead well.
- Divide the wheat flour dough into 6 equal balls.
- Dust the pastry board (*polpaat*) with rice flour and roll out 2 wheat dough balls into small discs the size of a *puri*, one slightly larger than the other.
- Place the gram flour-jaggery mixture between the 2 *poli* and press down lightly. Roll out into a thin *poli* making sure the jaggery has spread evenly to the edges. Trim off excess dough along the edges with a pastry cutter.
- Heat a *tawa* and roast the *poli* on a low heat till crisp.

Note: The *poli* is rolled really thin and the jaggery has a tendency to ooze out when hot, so making gool *poli* is not for the faint-hearted. One of the few people I know who actually make a good *gool poli* is my husband's neighbour in Pune who used to send us this lip-smacking delicacy every Holi.

Sanzachya Polya

FLATBREADS WITH SWEET SEMOLINA FILLING

Sanza is a sweet or savoury dish made out of semolina. The sweet version is better known as *sheera*, and can be used as a filling in *poli* for a tasty tea-time snack, or a convenient dish to eat while travelling.

Ingredients

Poli

1 cup wholewheat flour
2 tablespoons oil + for greasing
A pinch of salt
Rice flour, for dusting

Sheera

1 tablespoon ghee (*toop*)
1 cup semolina
⅔ cup grated jaggery
¼ teaspoon cardamom powder
2-3 saffron threads

Method

- For the *poli*, mix together the wheat flour, 2 tablespoons oil and salt and knead to make a smooth pliable dough. Set aside, covered, for at least 1 hour.
- For the *sheera*, heat the ghee on a *tawa* and lightly roast the semolina.
- Place the jaggery in a pan; add ⅔ cup of water, and dissolve the jaggery on medium heat. Add the cardamom and saffron and mix well.
- When the jaggery dissolves and the water comes to a boil, add the roasted semolina, mix well, and cook on low heat for 2-3 minutes. Remove from heat. Cool and divide into 12 equal portions. Set aside.
- Divide the dough into 12 equal portions and roll into balls.
- To make the *poli*, dip each ball in the oil and flatten into a thin disc with your fingers.
- Place 1 portion of the *sheera* on the disc, gather the edges together to enclose the filling.
- Sprinkle rice flour on a pastry board (*polpaat*) and flatten the stuffed dough ball into a patty. Roll out into a thin 4 to 6-inch *poli*.
- Heat the *tawa* and roast the *poli* drizzling 1 teaspoon oil. Roast on both sides till done.

Satorya

FLATBREADS WITH RICH SEMOLINA FILLING

Satorya are slightly different from Sanzachya Polya (page 139) because of the milk solids (*khava*) that are added to the filling. They are also thicker than *sanzachya polya*.

Ingredients

1 cup wholewheat flour
2 tablespoons oil + for drizzling
A pinch of salt
1 recipe Sheera (page 209)
¼ cup milk solids (*khava*)
Rice flour, for dusting

Method

- For the *poli*, knead together the wheat flour, 2 tablespoons oil and salt into an elastic dough, cover and set aside.
- Divide the dough into 12 equal balls.
- Dip each ball in some oil and flatten into a thin disc with your fingers.
- In a bowl, mix together the *sheera* and milk solids.
- Divide the *sheera* mixture into 12 equal portions and place 1 portion on each disc, gather the edges together to enclose the filling.
- Sprinkle rice flour on a pastry board (*polpaat*) and flatten the stuffed dough ball into a patty. Roll out into a thick 2 to 3-inch round *poli*.
- Heat a *tawa*. Place the *poli* on the *tawa*, drizzle a little oil around the edges and cook for a few seconds.
- Lower the heat and flip the *poli* over; drizzle a little oil around the edges, and cook until both sides are evenly browned. Remove and set aside to cool on absorbent paper.

Pakatlya Purya

SUGAR-COATED FRIED BREADS

This is a sweet *puri*, which is made on special occasions like a birthday, or even during *Shraavan*.

Ingredients

2 cups fine semolina or
1 cup refined flour + 1 cup fine semolina
½ cup sour yoghurt
A pinch of salt
1 tablespoon hot oil
Ghee (*toop*) for deep-frying

Sugar syrup

3 cups sugar
2-3 saffron threads
½ teaspoon cardamom powder

Method

- For the sugar syrup, cook the sugar with 1½ cups of water in a pan till the sugar dissolves and the syrups thickens to a 2-string consistency. Add the saffron and powdered cardamom. Keep warm.
- For the *puri*, mix together the flour, semolina, yoghurt, salt and hot oil, and knead to a stiff dough. Set aside for 10 minutes. Divide the dough into lime-sized balls.
- Roll the balls out into 4-inch discs.
- Heat the ghee in a *kadai* and deep-fry the *puri*.
- Dip the hot *puri* in the hot syrup until well coated with the syrup.
- Serve warm, or cool and store in an airtight container for 4-5 days.

Gharge

PUMPKIN FLATBREADS

I always associate these *puri* with rainy days when I would come home from school to the aroma of *gharge* frying. They were the yummiest snack on a wet day with the *puri* just slightly sweet and the jaggery oozing out at the edges.

Ingredients

1 cup boiled mashed pumpkin
Wholewheat flour, as required
Salt to taste
Jaggery, as required
Oil for deep-frying

Method

- Add as much wheat flour as the mashed pumpkin can hold along with the salt and jaggery and knead to a stiff dough.
- Divide the dough into lime-sized balls.
- Grease a lightly greased pastry board and roll out the balls into thin discs.
- Heat the oil in a *kadai* and gently lower the discs into the oil. Lower the heat and deep-fry the *gharge* till they puff up and rise to the surface like small balloons.
- Remove and drain on absorbent paper.

Upahaar

SNACKS

Batatyachi Bhaji

POTATO FRITTERS

Ingredients

1 cup gram flour
¼-½ teaspoon salt
¼ teaspoon turmeric powder
¼ teaspoon red chilli powder
¼ teaspoon carom seeds (*owa*)
1 teaspoon hot oil
3 potatoes, peeled and sliced

Method

- Mix together the gram flour, salt, turmeric powder, chilli powder and carom seeds. Add the hot oil to make the batter light. Add enough water to make a thick batter.
- Dip the potato slices into the batter and coat well, and deep-fry in a *kadai* until crisp and brown. Drain off excess oil and serve hot with Hirvi Chutney (page 99).

Batate Wade

SPICY DEEP-FRIED POTATO DUMPLINGS

This all-time popular snack has been immortalised by street vendors in Mumbai and is so widely available that most people have even forgotten that this was once a home-made treat.

Ingredients

500 g potatoes
4-5 garlic cloves
2-3 green chillies
2 tablespoons finely chopped onion
1 tablespoon chopped coriander
Juice of ½ lime
Salt to taste
1 cup gram flour
¼ teaspoon turmeric powder
1 tablespoon oil + for deep-frying

Method

- Wash the potatoes and cook in a pressure cooker with 1½ cups of water till the pressure is released 5 times (5 whistles). Remove from heat, drain and cool. Peel and mash the potatoes until smooth.
- Grind together the garlic and green chillies to a paste.
- In a bowl, combine the mashed potato, garlic and green chilli paste, chopped onion, coriander, lime juice and salt to taste and mix well. Divide the potato mixture into 14 balls and flatten them slightly. For the batter, place the gram flour in a bowl, and add the turmeric powder, salt to taste and 1 tablespoon oil and mix well to make a smooth batter.
- Heat the oil in a *kadai*. Dip the potato balls in the batter and deep-fry on low heat. Turn them over from time to time with a slotted spoon, until golden brown. Drain on absorbent paper and serve with Hirvi Chutney (page 99).

Note: In another variation of this *wada*, which has largely been popularised by Joshi Wadewale of Pune, and immortalised in the iconic *wada pav*, fry mustard seeds in a little oil and add to the mashed potato along with finely chopped ginger. Onions are omitted in this version; in addition a pinch of sodium bicarbonate is added to the batter, so that the outside covering is thicker and spongier than the thin crisp covering of the traditional *wada*.

Kandyachi Bhaji

DEEP-FRIED FRITTERS

While *bhaji* are a traditional favourite, and a must on special occasions, they were my introduction to cooking and will, therefore, hold a special place in my heart. I will always associate them with the Home Science class I used to attend as a 14-year old. Particularly in the monsoons, their crispy crunchiness is the perfect accompaniment to hot tea.

Ingredients

2-3 onions, finely sliced
2 cups gram flour or as required
1 teaspoon carom seeds
Salt to taste
½ teaspoon turmeric powder
½ teaspoon red chilli powder
1 tablespoon hot oil + for deep-frying

Method

- Separate the sliced onion segments.
- Add as much gram flour as required to cling to the onion, together with the carom seeds, salt, turmeric powder, chilli powder and hot oil. Carefully mix everything together with the hand.
- Heat the oil in a *kadai* and gently drop small clumps of the mixture into the hot oil. Deep-fry until golden brown.
- Drain on absorbent paper.
- Serve piping hot with Hirvi Chutney (page 99).

Note: Fritters can also be made with bottle gourd, spinach leaves, and oregano leaves. While making fritters with carom leaves omit the oregano seeds.

Dhirda

SAVOURY GRAM FLOUR PANCAKES

Traditionally a *dhirda* is made out of all the flours that one has on hand, especially a mix of rice flour and gram flour, but I would like to share the recipe of my husband's favourite breakfast dish, which has only gram flour. *Dhirda* is a pancake and is much thicker than a *dosa*.

Ingredients

2 cups gram flour
1 tablespoon hot oil + 2 tablespoons oil for drizzling
¼ teaspoon turmeric powder
¼ teaspoon red chilli powder
Salt to taste
½ onion, finely chopped
2 garlic cloves, finely chopped
1 teaspoon finely chopped coriander

Method

- Place the gram flour in a bowl and add the hot oil, turmeric powder, chilli powder, salt and water. Mix well to make a smooth batter of pouring consistency. A wire whisk helps break up the lumps.
- Add the onion, garlic, and coriander to the batter.
- Heat a tawa. For each *dhirda*, pour one-fourth of the batter onto the *tawa* and carefully move the *tawa* in a circular motion to spread the batter evenly. Lower the heat and drizzle oil around the edges of the *dhirda*.
- When the edges start leaving the *tawa*, flip the *dhirda* over and cook the other side.
- Serve with Hirvi Chutney (page 99).

Note: My mother's recipe calls for 1 cup of gram flour and ½ cup of rice flour. This is also known as a 'vegetarian omelette', and can be made with some chopped tomatoes thrown in.

Paangi

STEAMED RICE PANCAKES

These mildly flavoured rice pancakes are a dieter's delight since they are almost fat-free. Particularly welcome on a rainy afternoon, they can also be eaten as a light snacky dinner or lunch. Ideally, they should be steamed in turmeric leaves, but since the leaves are hard to come by, a banana leaf will do. Of course in its modern day *avatar*, you could perhaps also try making them in a non-stick frying pan, spreading them in the shape of a 'cat's tongue' instead of a round pancake.

Ingredients

2 cups rice flour

½ cup yoghurt, mixed with water into a thick buttermilk (*taak*)

1½ teaspoons salt

1 teaspoon cumin seeds

¼ teaspoon asafoetida (*hing*)

1 teaspoon oil

Fresh green chilli paste (optional)

Fresh ginger paste (optional)

2-3 banana leaves

Method

- Wash, clean, and wipe the banana leaves dry. Depending on the size of the leaf, cut into 3 to 4 parts.
- Mix the rice flour into the *taak* and add salt, cumin seeds and asafoetida to make a batter of dropping consistency.
- Add the oil to the batter to ensure that the *paangi* remain soft.
- At this stage you may add freshly ground green chilli and/or freshly ground ginger paste to taste.
- Spread some batter on one half of each piece of banana leaf and fold the other half over to cover the batter.
- Heat a *tawa*; place the *paangi* on the hot *tawa* and cook evenly on both sides, until the leaves start turning brown.
- Uncover and serve the *paangi* with fresh Hirvi Chutney (page 99).

Note: This quantity of batter will make 15-20 *paangi* (depending on how thin or thick you like them), and should be more than enough for 6 people.

Dadpe Pohe

NO-COOK SPICED RICE FLAKES

Similar to the regular *pohe*, this is even easier to make because it is not cooked!

Ingredients

1 cup wafer-thin rice flakes (*patal pohe*)
1 medium onion, finely chopped
1-2 green chillies, finely chopped
Salt to taste
Sugar to taste
1 tablespoon lime juice
1 tablespoon finely chopped coriander
1 tablespoon grated coconut

Seasoning

1 tablespoon oil
½ teaspoon mustard seeds
¼ teaspoon turmeric powder
2-3 curry leaves

Method

- Wash the rice flakes under running water and leave to drain in a colander for around 10-15 minutes to make them light and fluffy.
- Transfer the rice flakes to a bowl. Add the chopped onion, chillies, salt and sugar and mix well.
- For the seasoning, heat the oil in a *kadai* and add the mustard seeds. When they start to splutter, add the turmeric powder and curry leaves.
- Pour the seasoning over the rice flakes, add the lime juice and mix well.
- Serve hot, garnished with chopped coriander and grated coconut.

Dahi Pohe

SPICED RICE FLAKES WITH YOGHURT

Akin to Dahi Bhaat (page 46), this is another traditional recipe for *pohe*, and is usually made to celebrate Gopalkala, the day after Janmashtami or Gokul Ashtami (Lord Krishna's birthday).

Ingredients

1 cup thick rice flakes
1 medium onion (optional), finely chopped
1-2 green chillies, finely chopped
½ cup yoghurt
Salt to taste
Sugar to taste
1 tablespoon finely chopped coriander

Seasoning

1 tablespoon oil
¼ teaspoon mustard seeds
2-3 curry leaves

Method

- Wash the rice flakes under running water and leave to drain in a colander for around 10-15 minutes. This makes them light and fluffy.
- Add the chopped onion and green chillies to the rice flakes. Add the yoghurt, salt and sugar and mix well.
- For the seasoning, heat the oil in a *kadai* and add the mustard seeds. When they start to splutter, add the curry leaves.
- Pour the seasoning onto the rice flakes. Mix well.
- Serve, garnished with chopped coriander.

Note: These *pohe* cannot be made too much ahead of time as they will become soft and mushy.

Kaande Batate Pohe

SPICED RICE FLAKES WITH POTATO AND ONION

This is the way *pohe* are traditionally made. This dish can really be made in a jiffy and is normally offered to guests who drop by unexpectedly, especially around tea-time.

Ingredients

1 cup thick rice flakes
1-2 green chillies, finely chopped
1 medium onion, finely chopped
1 medium potato, quartered and thinly sliced
Salt to taste
Sugar to taste
A squeeze of lime, to taste
1 tablespoon chopped coriander
1 tablespoon grated coconut

Seasoning

1 tablespoon oil
¼ teaspoon mustard seeds
¼ teaspoon turmeric powder
2-3 curry leaves

Method

- Wash the rice flakes under running water and leave to drain in a colander for 10-15 minutes. This makes them light and fluffy.
- Heat oil in a pan and add the mustard seeds. When they start to splutter, add turmeric powder, curry leaves, chopped chillies and onion. Lower the heat and stir till the onion turns pink.
- Add the chopped potato and stir in the salt. Cook, covered, till potato turns soft.
- When the potato is done, add the rice flakes and give it a good stir making sure that all the ingredients are well mixed. Cover and simmer for 1-2 minutes.
- Stir in some sugar and a squeeze of lime. Take off the heat and serve garnished with chopped coriander and fresh grated coconut.

Tikhat Mithacha Sanza

SEMOLINA SAVOURY

Also known as, *upma*, this savoury semolina dish can be made into a substantial meal by adding vegetables like peas, tomatoes, diced carrots and soaked cashew nuts. Depending on whether you like your *upma* gooey or dryish, you can vary the quantity of water, but basically one should add 1½ times the amount of semolina used.

Ingredients

1 cup semolina
1 small onion, finely chopped
½ medium tomato, chopped (optional)
1-2 green chillies, finely chopped
½ cup shelled green peas (optional)
2-3 cashew nuts, soaked in a little water
Salt to taste
Juice of ½ lime
1 tablespoon finely chopped coriander
1 tablespoon grated coconut

Seasoning

1 tablespoon oil
¼ teaspoon mustard seeds
2-3 curry leaves

Method

- Dry- roast the semolina in a *kadai* till it turns slightly pinkish brown and fragrant. Transfer to a dish and set aside. For the seasoning, heat the oil in a *kadai* and add mustard seeds. When they start to splutter, add the curry leaves and chopped onion.
- Lower the heat and sauté the onion till soft. At this stage, you can also add the chopped tomato, green chillies, green peas, along with the soaked cashew nuts.
- Add 1½ cups of water, salt, and lime juice and bring to a boil.
- When the water starts bubbling, add the roasted semolina, lower the heat, and cook, covered, for 5 minutes, till the water has been absorbed. Mix well.
- Serve hot, garnished with chopped coriander and grated coconut.

Appe

STEAMED SEMOLINA CAKES

Appe are cooked in a strange looking utensil which is the traditional cast iron utensil called *appe patra*. Unlike the *idli* which requires at least 12 hours of fermentation, *appe* or steamed semolina cakes take realatively less time to make. Besides, they can be cooked within minutes, and served piping hot.

Ingredients

1 cup semolina
½ cup yoghurt
¼ teaspoon cumin seeds
½ teaspoon salt
½ teaspoon finely chopped ginger
1 teaspoon finely chopped coriander
1 teaspoon finely chopped green chillies
Ghee (*toop*) or oil for greasing

Method

- Mix together all the ingredients in a bowl, except the ghee, to make a batter of spreading consistency. Cover and set aside to ferment for at least 4 hours.
- Wash, wipe dry and grease the *appe patra*.
- Heat the *appe patra*, pour the batter into each of the 7 moulds, lower the heat and cook, covered for 5 minutes.
- You can turn the *appe* over in the moulds and cook again for 2 minutes.
- When the *appe* are done and slightly browned, they will easily slip out of the moulds.
- Serve hot with Hirvi Chutney (page 99).

Note: Yoghurt can be substituted with buttermilk, but make sure that the batter is not too thin and runny.

Khaas Padartha

FOOD FOR IMPORTANT OCCASIONS

This chapter deals with all the festivals that are mentioned in the traditional calendar that hangs in most *Kokanastha* homes. Many festivals are not celebrated, but still get a mention in the calendar, so they are mentioned in this section as well.

Kokanasthas, like all Hindus, follow the lunar calendar and celebrate each day according to the movement of the stars and planets charted out all those hundreds of years ago and tabulated according to the ephemerides or phases of the moon. Printed every year, this almanac marks out the days and their significance and is commonly found in every home as a *Kaalnirnay* or *Panchang* and are often to before starting out on something new, going on a journey or even having a surgical procedure! These calendars not only keep track of the tides and the phases of the moon, but also tell us what is being celebrated, commemorated or honoured on a particular day.

CELEBRATING FESTIVALS FOR THE FIRST TIME

The first year of a child's life is very special not only for the child but also for the family. Hence, every festival for that first year has a special significance and is often marked by a special gift to the child from the parents or grandparents. Finally, when the child turns one, the family has a grand celebration surrounded by family and friends. Today a child's first birthday may have lost some of its significance, but in the past when infant mortality was high, this milestone event was worth commemorating.

Similarly, the festivals in a bride's first year of marriage are also of special significance. In days of yore, it was a daunting experience for a child bride to leave her family and go to a new home. Imagine starting a life in the company of virtual strangers. One way of making the new bride comfortable and easing her into her new home was to invite her family to every major festival celebration or send her to her maternal home to celebrate festivals during the first year of her marriage. Today, even though brides are no longer girls, this tradition is still maintained, and for many a bride her first Diwali after marriage, the *Manglagour*, *Chaitra haldi-kunku* remain special occasions to be cherished.

Gudi Padva: Shrikhand (page 183)

Ramnavmi: Sunthavda for *prasad*

Akshay Tritiya: Aamras, Ambyacha Bhaat (page 49)

Kande Navmi: Kande Bhaat

Ashadhi Ekadashi: Fasting Food

Jiwiti: Puran Poli (page 136)

Naarali Poornima: Naarali Bhaat (page 48)

Gopalkala: Dahi Pohe (savoury) (page 149)

Hartalika: Fasting Food

Ganesh Chaturthi: Modak with jaggery (page 175)

Rishipanchami: Special *Rishichi bhaji* –5 vegetables not cultivated by cattle

Gauri Ganpati: Ghavan Ghatla (page 177, 178), Doodh Gool Shevaiya (page 179)

Anant Chaturdashi: Sanzachya Polya (page 139)

Pithori Amavasya: Kheer (page 217)

Ghatasthapana (First day of Navratri): Puran Poli (page 136)

Navratri: *Patole*, *Laadoo*, Karanji (page 187), *Shevaiya kheer*, Puran Poli (page 136), Gharge (page 142), Satorya (page 140)

Dussera: Baasundi (page 156)

Kojagiri Poornima: Masala Doodh (page 184), Khamang Kakdichi Koshimbir (page 103)

Diwali: Sheera Puri (page 209, 132) and *pharaal*

Balipratipada: Shrikhand (page 183) /Baasundi (page 156)

Bhaubeej: Anything the brother likes

Dattajayanti: Upvas

Bhogi: Bajri Bhaakri (page 133) with sesame seeds, and *Bhogichi Bhaaji*

Sankrant: Gool Poli (page 138), Teelache Laadoo (page 196)

Mahashivratri: Sabudanyachi Khichadi (page 163)

Holi: Puran Poli (page 136)

Chaitra (Mid March-Mid April)

GUDI PADVA

I always wondered why the whole world brings in the New Year on the first of January when most of the world is clouded in mist and winter chill. Wouldn't it seem more logical to celebrate the sprouting of fresh young leaves on the trees, in the crisp March air when the sun moves into Aries heralding new beginnings as the New Year? Spring time, with yet another cycle of sowing and reaping, is a welcome relief from the preceding cold winter months and it is no wonder then that the Hindu calendar begins with *Chaitra*, the first month of the Lunar Calendar, when the mellow sun begins to turn warm. The first day of the year is celebrated with much joy as it not only marks the New Year, but also the start of the Shalivahan Shak era in 78 AD and the Hindu calendar. Shalivahan was the grandson of the mighty King Vikramaditya who united all the southern tribes under one flag. To mark this occasion, we hoist the *gudi* (rather like a flag) outside our homes or in prominent places within the home. The *gudi* consists of a brightly coloured silk cloth (preferably new) mounted on a pole and crowned with an inverted *tambya* or water tumbler. A garland of flowers, a bunch of Margosa (*neem*) or mango leaves and a specially crafted garland of sugar sweets (which are later on gobbled up by the children of the house) are used to decorate the *gudi* which is brought down at sunset. The *Padva* (or first day of the fortnight) is known as *Gudi Padva*. It is one of the three and a half days in our calendar along with *Akshay Trittiya, Dussera* and the *Padva* of Diwali that guarantees the success of any venture begun on that day.

The day begins with the traditional early morning bath, after which the household gathers to pray to Lord Brahma, the only time in the year that He is thus venerated. The four-headed Lord Brahma is represented by a coconut sitting atop a bed of mango leaves placed on a *kalash* or pot of water and placed in a quiet northward facing corner of the house. Thus installed, Lord Brahma is worshipped and the *prasad* or ritualistic offering of the bitter leaves of the *neem* tree (which is medicinal), and sugar (to tone down the bitterness) is distributed to all present to ensure good health all the year long.

People dress up in fresh new clothes, decorate the entrance of the house with *rangoli* (an intricate design fashioned with coloured powders) and festoon the doorway with a garland of mango leaves and marigolds. The special sweet made to mark this auspicious beginning is a thick, creamy *baasundi* eaten with piping hot *puri*.

Baasundi

SWEETENED EVAPORATED MILK

Ingredients

2 litres milk
2 cups sugar
½ teaspoon powdered cardamom
A pinch of saffron threads
1 teaspoon *cudpah* nuts (*chironji*)
1 teaspoon slivered almonds

Method

- Heat the milk in a heavy-bottomed pan, stirring occasionally, to prevent the milk from scorching, till it reduces to one-third the original quantity. If you feel this is too thick, you can reduce it to half the original quantity.
- Once the milk is of the desired consistency, add the sugar and stir till dissolved.
- Add the powdered cardamom, saffron, *cudpah* nuts and almonds. Leave to cool and place in a refrigerator to chill.
- Serve chilled with hot Puri (page 132).

Note: I must warn you that reducing the fresh milk is a time-consuming activity and it can be substituted with condensed milk, but the aroma of cardamom and saffron, and the thick creamy consistency of a smoky-flavoured, slightly caramelised baasundi is unparalleled and worth the extra effort!

RAMNAVMI

Our calendar has two *Navratri* or Festivals of Nine Nights. The first *Navratri* which is celebrated in the first half of the year culminates in the celebration of Lord Rama's birthday which is on the ninth day of this month. This festival is not celebrated in Maharashtra but merits a mention in our calendar.

VASANT GAURI

Gauri, the Goddess of Prosperity, is believed to come back to her maternal home for an annual month-long holiday and is welcomed into our homes on the third day of *Chaitra*. For this one month, the lady of the house specially honours Gauri during her daily worship, and makes an extra sweet dish in her honour every day. This occasion is also celebrated with friends and family, when married women and their daughters are invited to a *haldi-kunku* (named for turmeric which is an auspicious spice, and vermilion which is used on the forehead by married women) a social event for married women. Much looked forward to in the days when women were mainly homebodies, this event is gradually losing its importance and is seldom celebrated today. However, it still remains a good way to introduce a young bride to the friends of her new family, and is a definite way of getting all the women to attend as it is considered inauspicious to decline an invitation to such a function.

The function can be as simple or as fancy as desired, the main requirement being the actual exchange of *haldi-kunku* by the married women present. Today, this distinction is not rigidly followed and all the women present irrespective of their marital status are given *haldi* and *kunku*. As the women begin streaming in, they are welcomed with garlands of *mogra* (jasmine) or a single rose to put in their hair. This task is normally relegated to the little girls who also love splashing the guests with rose water and dabbing *attar* on their hands, while the hostess applies one dot each of *halad* and *kunku* on the guests' forehead.

Haldi-kunku ceremonies are held either at homes or in community halls. For the *Chaitra haldi-kunku*, a handful of fresh green *harbara* or green gram and a small gift are placed in the outspread padar or *saree pallu* of each guest. The gift is usually a kitchen utensil or gadget, fabric for a *saree* blouse or something of utility. A must on the menu is *ambyachi dal*, green mango juice (*panha*) or sugarcane juice, chopped cucumber and watermelon.

Apart from *Chaitra, haldi-kunku* can be held at other times as well: to introduce the new bride to all the mother-in-law's friends, or show off the young girls of the home to 'prospective mothers-in-law'! It is also a good way to celebrate *Sankranti*, and welcome Gauri home during the Ganesh festival. The menu for the *Chaitra haldi-kunku* follows.

Ambyachi Dal

NO-COOK SPICED SPLIT GRAM WITH MANGO

Our ancestors were very wise, for not only did they have pre-determined menus for every occasion, they also had menus that were easy to manage. For instance, *ambyachi dal* which is made of spiced up raw split Bengal gram, doesn't particularly require any skill or aptitude, and doesn't require any last minute work. Therefore, once you make a whole load of it, you can happily go ahead and enjoy your evening with your guests at the *haldi-kunku*.

Ingredients

1 kg split Bengal gram (*chana dal*)
1-2 unripe mangoes, peeled and finely grated
1 green chilli, finely chopped (optional)
Salt to taste
Freshly grated coconut
Freshly chopped coriander

Seasoning

1-2 teaspoons oil
¼ teaspoon mustard seeds
½ teaspoon turmeric powder
¼ teaspoon asafoetida (*hing*)
2-3 curry leaves
1 red chilli

Method

- Soak the *dal* for a few hours. Wash and drain.
- Coarsely grind the *dal* and add the grated mango and salt.
- For the seasoning, heat the oil in a pan and add the mustard seeds. When they start to splutter, add turmeric powder, asafoetida, curry leaves and red chilli.
- Pour the seasoning over the *dal*, and garnish with chopped coriander and grated coconut.

Note: Those who like their food particularly pungent can add a green chilli while grinding the *dal*. The sourness can be increased with a squeeze of lime if desired.

Panha

GREEN MANGO REFRESHER

This refreshing sweet and sour drink with a hint of cardamom and saffron, is a harbinger of the unparalleled sweetness of an Alphonso mango summer, and no amount of aerated or fancy drinks can ever replace the joy of *panha*.

Ingredients

½ kg or 3-4 unripe mangoes
2 cups sugar
Salt to taste
1 teaspoon powdered cardamom
A pinch of saffron threads

Method

- Pressure-cook the unripe mangoes till the pressure is released 3 times (3 whistles). When the skin splits open, it is a sign that the mangoes are cooked enough.
- Peel the mangoes, and squeeze out the pulp and blend to a smooth paste in a blender.
- Transfer the pulp to a pan; add sugar, salt, cardamom and saffron and cook till the sugar dissolves. This is the *panha* concentrate.
- Dilute the *panha* concentrate in water adjusting the amount of water and sugar until you get the desired tangy sweetness.

Note: While *ambyachi dal* and *panha* are a must for the *Chaitra haldi-kunku*, other dishes like Batate Wade (page 144), Kaande Batate Pohe (page 150), Sabudana Wada (page 162) etc, can also be served.

Vaishakh (Mid April-Mid May)

With the sun making its way into the house of the bull or Taurus, temperatures begin to rise. By this time of year, which is around the middle of May, schools generally close for the summer holidays, and it is time to celebrate with mangoes, weddings and sacred thread ceremonies (*munjas*).

AKSHAY TRITIYA

On this last day of the Vasant Gauri festival (which is also third day of *Vaishakh*) when the Goddess *Gauri* returns to her marital home, the sun and moon are simultaneously at their shiniest best. This day can be crudely translated as 'the eternal day of good luck'. This day also happens to be the birthday of Parshuram and is of special significance to *Kokanasthas*.

While there is no particular ceremony, ritual or food associated with this day, it is normally celebrated with the purchase of gold coins or jewellery. Since it is also one of the 3½ auspicious moments, several weddings, thread ceremonies, inaugurations of factories or shop openings and *pooja* are held on this day as well. *Aamras puri* made of the best Alphonso mangoes is served on the occasion.

Jyestha (Mid May-Mid June)

Continuing its celestial journey the sun enters the constellation of Gemini bringing in its wake the early monsoon clouds.

VATA POORNIMA

The festival that celebrates the devotion and duty of Savitri, the wife of Satyavan is celebrated on the full moon day of Jyestha. Everyone knows the story of Savitri who refused to let go of her husband Satyavan to Yama, the God of death, and followed him to the gates of the Nether World. Impressed by her wifely devotion, Yama told Savitri that much as he would like to restore Satyavan to her, he could not but, recognising her great devotion he was willing to grant her one wish. Savitri very cleverly wished for a son and her wish was granted. Then, after thanking Yama for the gift, told him that she could not have a son without a husband! Thus, caught in a trap of his own making, Yama had no option but to restore Satyavan to Savitri.

Now the banyan tree is supposed to be ageless and eternal, so this legend is celebrated by fasting and tying a cotton thread around the tree while going around it seven times, signifying the seven lifetimes of being married to the same man. Unlike the normal festival fare, this festival calls for food specially eaten on a fast: fruit or milk and milk products.

Ashaadh (Mid June-Mid July)

With the rains pouring down really hard and everyone busy in the fields, Lord Vishnu, Protector of the World, takes a break and begins his four-month long slumber. So the ladies of the house begin their *Chaturmas* or a four-month period of fasting and penance to keep all evil influences at bay, with *Kaanda Navmi*, which is the last day they are permitted to eat onions before the start of *Chaturmas*, two days later on.

ASHAADHI EKADASHI

While the whole of Maharashtra observes this special fast, the sleepy town of Pandharpur on the banks of the river Chandrabhaga, comes to life when thousands of pilgrims who begin their journey on foot from Alandi 120 km away, converge on the temple of Lord Vitthal or Vithoba, (the Lord who Stands on a Brick) or Vishnu, as he is worshipped in Maharashtra.

Conventionally, it rains cats and dogs on that day, and while the rest of the world is scurrying around in the pelting rain, those of us who are at home can savour the aroma of *toop* and all the glorious calories that go into the 'fasting' food with which we celebrate this day.

Fasting, actually is willingly abstaining from everyday food, and people fast according to their personal preferences. Several people fast every *Sankashti* (the fourth day in the dark half of the fortnight), or on *Ekadashi* (the eleventh day), or *Poornima* (full moon nights), during special periods like *Navratri*, or on days of the week dedicated to certain Gods (Monday is the day of Lord Shiva or Shankar, Tuesday is Lord Ganesh's day, Thursday is the day of Lord Dattatreya, Friday is the day of the Mother Goddess and Saturday the day of Lord Hanuman and Shani). I realised quite late in life that many women use this excuse to keep away from regular food and often substitute fasting food with a more healthy option like fresh fruit and milk products thus keeping their weight down! This varying of diet is often suggested by modern dieticians. Whatever the motive for fasting, it is undoubtedly a break from regular food and the whole household winds up observing the fast, if not for the religious sentiment, at least for the sake of a baser instinct – the desire for good food. The fast is generally from sunrise to sunset, but can also be observed by eating just one major meal in the day, and fasting for half the day. The essential ingredients in the shopping list for 'fasting food' are non-cereal foods, such as sago (*sabudana*), potatoes, coconut, peanuts, ghee and cumin seeds. If you notice, most of the foods that are acceptable in a fast are not native to India which always prompts my father to ask, "What did people eat during a fast before the potato?"

Sabudana Wada

FRIED SAGO PATTIES

Sabudana or pearl sago is actually made from starch from the tapioca root, which came to India from Brazil. Considering the distinctly un-Indian origins of this ingredient, I cannot imagine how this became part of our food for fasting, but Indian or otherwise, one cannot ignore its particularly delicious taste. *Sabudana* looks like small homeopathic pills, and can only be cooked when rehydrated. Since this is essentially pure starch (or almost), it cannot be soaked in water, but washed carefully and then allowed to fluff up in a covered colander or sieve.

Ingredients

1 cup sago
½ cup mashed potato
Salt to taste
A pinch of sugar
½ cup roasted peanut powder
1 teaspoon cumin powder
1-2 green chillies, finely chopped
1 tablespoon finely chopped coriander
1 cup ghee (*toop*) for deep-frying

Method

- Rehydrate the sago by washing it in three changes of water in a colander. Drain the water completely, cover and set aside for at least 4 hours.
- To the sago, add the mashed potato, salt, sugar, peanut powder, cumin powder, chillies and chopped coriander. Divide the sago mixture into five to six portions and shape them into patties (*wade*).
- Heat the ghee in a *kadai* and deep-fry the *wade*. Serve piping hot.

Sabudanyachi Khichadi

SPICY SAGO SAVOURY

Unlike regular *khichadi*, this is made out of sago and is extremely popular as a teatime snack as well. It can also be served for breakfast on *Satyanarayan pooja* days, at weddings or thread ceremonies, or on any day that requires one to fast before a *pooja*.

Ingredients

1 cup sago (*sabudana*)
1 tablespoon ghee (*toop*)
1 teaspoon cumin seeds
1 potato, thinly sliced
Salt to taste
1-2 green chillies, finely chopped
½ cup coarsely ground roasted peanuts
A pinch of sugar
Juice of ½ a lime
1 tablespoon chopped fresh coriander
1 tablespoon grated fresh coconut

Method

- Rehydrate the sago by washing it thrice in a colander. Drain the water completely, cover and set aside for at least 4 hours. For the fluffiest *khichadi*, the sago should be allowed to rest overnight.
- For the seasoning, heat the ghee in a *kadai* and add the cumin seeds. When they start to splutter, add the sliced potato, salt and green chillies. Stir well, and cook, covered, on low heat.
- Place the sago in a bowl. Add the ground peanuts, salt, and sugar and mix well.
- Once the potatoes are soft, add the sago mixture and mix well. Add the lime juice and cook, covered, on low heat for 10 minutes.
- Garnish with chopped coriander and grated coconut and serve hot with yoghurt on the side.

Batatyacha Kees

GRATED SPICED POTATOES

A bit like hash browns, *batatyacha kees* is the easiest fasting food to make.

Ingredients

4 medium potatoes, peeled and grated
½ cup roasted peanut powder
2-3 tablespoons ghee (*toop*)
½ teaspoon cumin seeds
1 green chilli, chopped
Salt to taste
A pinch of sugar
1 tablespoon chopped coriander

Method

- Squeeze out the excess starch from the grated potatoes and drain well.
- Add peanut powder to the potatoes and mix.
- Heat the ghee in a pan and add the cumin seeds, and chopped chillies and sauté for a few seconds.
- Then add the potato and peanuts, salt and a pinch of sugar. Stir well and cook, covered, on low heat for a few minutes. Within minutes the potatoes will be done. Drain on absorbent paper.
- Add the chopped green coriander and serve with yoghurt.

Note: This dish can also be made out of sweet potatoes. Alternatively, this mix can be flattened like a pancake on a griddle, covered and allowed to cook like *thalipeeth*, drizzling *toop* (ghee) from the side and flipping it once to cook evenly on both sides.

Daanyachi Aamti

PEANUT CURRY

Like Tweedledum and Tweedledee, *daanyachi* aamti and *varyache bhaat* are inseparable, and the staple of a major *upvas* like Ashadhi *Ekadashi* and *Mahashivratri*.

Ingredients

1 cup roasted peanuts
2 *kokum* rinds
1 tablespoon chopped fresh coriander
1 tablespoon grated fresh coconut

Spice paste

2-3 cloves
A small piece of cinnamon
½ teaspoon cumin powder
1-2 green chillies
Salt to taste
A pinch of sugar

Method

- Grind the peanut powder to a fine paste. Grind the ingredients for the spice paste separately.
- Bring 2 cups of water to a boil in pan and add the peanut paste.
- Add the spice paste and *kokum* and cook on low heat for 2-3 minutes.
- Serve, garnished with chopped coriander and grated coconut.

Varyacha Bhaat

SAMO SEED PULAO

This short-grained 'rice' is actually not rice but samo seeds (*vari tandul*). It is cooked like rice and served with Daanyachi Aamti (page 165). Alternatively, you can turn it into a *pulav*.

Ingredients

1 cup samo seeds (*vari tandul*)
2 tablespoons ghee (*toop*)
½ teaspoon cumin seeds
1 finely chopped green chilli (optional)
Salt to taste
1 teaspoon coriander, finely chopped

Method

- Wash and soak the samo seeds for about 10 minutes. Drain.
- Heat the ghee in a pan, and add the cumin seeds. When they start to splutter, add the samo seeds, and chopped chilli, and stir well for 1-2 minutes. Add double the quantity of water, salt to taste and cook on low heat till soft.
- Continue to cook covered for 2-3 minutes.
- Serve hot, garnished with chopped coriander.

Batatyachi Bhaaji

SPICED POTATOES

What differentiates this vegetable from its pedestrian cousin is the fact that it is made in ghee and minus the turmeric. But despite its pale, anaemic appearance, the addition of ghee and cumin seeds lifts it from the ordinary to the divine.

Ingredients

2 large potatoes
Salt to taste
1 tablespoon ghee (*toop*)
½ teaspoon cumin seeds, ground
1 finely chopped green chilli
1 tablespoon chopped fresh coriander
1 tablespoon grated fresh coconut

Method

- Boil and peel the potatoes. Cut into large pieces and sprinkle with some salt.
- For the seasoning, heat the ghee in a pan and add the ground cumin seeds and fry for a few seconds. Then add the chilli and the potatoes. Stir well and cook till tender.
- Serve hot, garnished with chopped coriander and grated coconut.

Kharikachi Kheer

DRIED DATES IN COCONUT MILK

This is personally on my hate list but I am including this in the traditional *upvaasache jeyvan* (fasting foods).

Ingredients

1 cup dried dates (*kharik*)
1 cup coconut milk
2 tablespoons sugar

Method

- Chop the dried dates into fine slivers and soak in warm water, till soft.
- Place the dates in a pan and add the coconut milk. Cook on low heat taking care not to curdle the milk.
- Add sugar to taste. Mix well till the sugar dissolves and remove from the heat. Cool and serve chilled.

GURU POORNIMA

This is a special day when one remembers and honours one's teachers and mentors. There is no specific way of honouring a teacher, but it is indeed nice to remember them at least once in the year!

ASHAADH PAATTHI

I never really knew this custom existed till my sister-in-law told me that this is actually what she experienced during her first year of marriage. Traditionally, weddings took place in the month of May when schools and colleges were closed for an eight-week long vacation. This meant that by the time Aashadh came around, the bride had spent just about a month in her new home.

Thus, on the first day of Ashaadh, the girl's mother brings over saffron-coloured *sarees* to gift to the ladies of the house, and goodies made of mango, such as mango and coconut stuffed *karanji*, mango rice, mango *poli*, mango chutney and of course some Alphonso mangoes that will soon vanish with the impending rains! Like most customs this tradition has fallen by the wayside especially in urban households, but it is still followed in rural homes.

Hapoosachi Chutney

FRESH ALPHONSO MANGO CHUTNEY

The velvety sweetness of mango tinged with the zing of mustard is an amazing combination and will liven up any meal. This recipe calls for red mustard seeds which has a milder flavour.

Ingredients

½ teaspoon red mustard seeds, soaked overnight

¼ teaspoon turmeric powder

¼ teaspoon asafoetida (*hing*)

Salt to taste

1 cup diced ripe Alphonso mango

Method

- Grind the mustard seeds into a fine paste. Add turmeric powder and asafoetida to the paste.
- Lightly rub the paste on a plate with your fingers to work up a light, fluffy foam.
- Add the paste to the diced mango, with salt to taste and give it a good stir.

Aambyachi Aamti

CURRIED ALPHONSO MANGOES

Ingredients

1 ripe Alphonso mango, peeled

Seasoning

1 teaspoon oil
½ teaspoon mustard seeds
¼ teaspoon turmeric powder
2-3 curry leaves

Method

- Heat the oil in a pan and add the mustard seeds. When they start to splutter, add the turmeric powder and curry leaves and fry for a few seconds.
- Add the whole mango and 1 cup of water to the pan. Stir well and cook on low heat till done.

Shravan (Mid July-Mid August)

Considered to be the holiest month of the Hindu calendar, *Shravan* is dedicated to contemplation and prayer. Almost every day is dedicated to some deity, or is marked with some festivity. Mondays and Fridays are considered particularly auspicious. Most women folk observe a fast on Mondays, while Fridays are celebrated with a feast. I remember my mother inviting at least one married woman (*savashin*) every Friday to join us for a special lunch symbolising the visit of the Goddess Laxmi to our home. It is considered a great honour to be invited, and inauspicious to decline an invitation. Suffice to say that like all religious occasions, a lady should not be 'unclean' (menstruating) at that time. Strangely enough a married daughter qualifies to be a *shavashin* even if she is staying in her maternal home, because technically she belongs to another family, and a daughter-in-law, even if she lives a hundred miles away is not considered a stranger to the family, and will not be accepted as a guest.

Apart from the lunch which is a normal feast and must include *puran poli*, one should not forget to honour the *savashin* with *dakshina* (a cash gift, generally a token amount of Rs.1.25/-) and an *oti* or gift, that is placed in the outspread *padar* or *saree pallu*, consisting of a coconut and three fistfuls of rice, a piece of fabric for a *saree, haldi-kunku* and a *veni* (garland of flowers). The minimum one can offer a *savashin* is given just the *haldi-kunku* and the *dakshina*.

Incidentally, whenever a coconut is offered to a guest, it should be given with the pointed end facing the recipient. The *dakshina* is normally placed on two paan leaves (betel nut leaves), and a betel nut, and placed on the left side of the plate.

NAGPANCHAMI

With rivers in spate at this time of the year, the countryside is crawling with snakes and to safeguard against snake bites, we worship snakes on the fifth day of the month. On this particular day, no land is tilled, a knife is not used to chop food, and no food is cooked at home, for fear of inadvertently killing a snake. So people generally ate fresh fruit and milk and milk products. People worship clay idols of the King Cobra (which are later immersed), or images of the snake drawn with turmeric and red sandalwood paste.

According to the legend of *Nagpanchami*, a farmer accidentally killed nine baby snakes while tilling his land. The mother snake sought to avenge their killing, by biting the farmer and his family in the dark of the night. Unfortunately for the mother snake, the farmer's eldest daughter who was married escaped this fate, but the unforgiving mother snake went in search of her. Just as she was about to enter the girl's home and strike, she saw her praying before an image of a cobra, seeking forgiveness for any mistakes on her part and asking for protection for her and her family. The girl's devotion made Mother Snake repent her earlier action and she told the girl that her family could be brought back to life by sprinkling nectar on their bodies. Thus the farmer and his family regained their lives. Thus on the fifth day of *Shravan* we worship the King Cobra, by praying to a clay idol of a snake, and leaving a saucer of milk on the doorstep for the snakes to drink.

MANGALAGAUR POOJA

On the four Tuesdays of *Shravan*, newly-married women pray to the Mother Goddess seeking her blessings for a long, happy and prosperous married life. Traditionally the *Mangalagaur* is celebrated by the young bride along with her newly-married friends for the first five years of her marriage. Nowadays, *Mangalagaur* becomes one celebration too many, but should you decide to have one, you should remember that the last *Mangalagaur* should officially end by the girl giving her mother a *vaan* or a gift of a *saree*, a coconut, *halad-kunku*, and *paan-supari*.

Traditionally, the *pooja* consists of the girl praying to the same idol of the Goddess *Annapurna* that she worshipped during the *gaurihar* ceremony on her wedding day, praying for a long and happy married life. This custom is particularly observed by the *Brahmin* classes, with our *Kokanashtas* making the 16 *diva* (oil lamps) and the ornaments out of *puran* rather than the more commonplace wheat flour. The Goddess is worshipped with flowers and a special *aarti* with 16 *divas*. The girls performing the *pooja*, fast and stay up till late at night playing traditional games like *phugadi* and *kombdi* with other devotees and guests. On the next day, after the *pooja*, the fast is broken and the feast of *Manglagaur* is celebrated with a *haldi-kunku*, and a lavish spread including Matkichi Usal (page 92) and Karanji (page 187).

NAARALI POORNIMA

From *Naarali Poornima* or Coconut Day the monsoon begins to lose some of its fury and the seas become calm again. It is celebrated by casting a coconut into the sea and the special foods on this day are naturally made out of coconut, such as Naarali Bhaat (page 48) and *naarlachi wadi*.

Naarlachi Wadi

COCONUT FUDGE

Ingredients

1 coconut
1 cup sugar
½ teaspoon powdered cardamom
A pinch of saffron threads
½ cup milk

Method

- Grate the coconut making sure that only the white flesh is used. (Keeping in mind the parsimonious *Kokanastha* gene, the brown bits can be used to make chutney or *masala*).
- Using the measured grated coconut as a guide, make a syrup by using half the amount of water and quarter the amount of sugar in a pan. Make the syrup till it is sticky and acquires a one-thread consistency.
- Add cardamom powder and saffron and mix together.
- Add the grated coconut and ½ cup milk and continue to cook, stirring occasionally, until the mixture starts leaving the sides of the pan.
- Pour the cooked coconut mixture into a greased flat dish or baking tray and pat down with a greased spoon or spatula to spread evenly. Leave to set.
- Cut into cubes and serve.

Note: You can substitute the milk with ½ cup *mawa* instead, to make a richer *barfi*.

RAKHI POORNIMA

Rakhi is not really an important festival though it has assumed greater importance these days thanks to our exposure to modern Hindi cinema with its North Indian overtones. However, should you wish to celebrate it, a sister invites a brother to her home on this day, seeking his protection and rewards him by making sure he gets his favourite food.

GOKUL ASHTAMI

Gokul Ashtami is celebrated with traditional fasting and midnight prayers to commemorate the birth of Lord Krishna in Mathura. The following day is celebrated as *Dahi handi* where a clay pot suspened from a height and filled with puffed sorghum *lhaya* (popped sorghum grains) and yoghurt is knocked down by a young child representing the young Lord Krishna, whose favourite food was yoghurt. The *prasad* (sacred food) that tumbles out is eaten by everyone. Dahi Pohe (page 149) is one of the traditional dishes served on that day.

PITHORI AMAVASYA

This last day of *Shravan* is a very special day for mothers. Legend has it that several hundred years ago, a woman named Vaidehi used to deliver her babies year after year on this particular day, only to have them die in childbirth or soon after. After several stillbirths, her husband cast her out and a totally shattered Vaidehi wandered into the nearby forest and prayed desperately for her luck to turn. Luckily, 64 Gods heard her prayers and appeared before her and assured her that henceforth any child that she bore would not only survive but have a long and happy life. Thus assured, a happy Vaidehi returned home to her husband and eventually bore him eight strapping sons who lived a long, happy life. That is why on this day, mothers pray for the long lives of their children. Apart from her normal *pooja*, the mother offers special prayers to a picture of the *Jivti*, which is placed alongside the family gods on this day. The specialty sweet on this day is Puran Poli (page 136) and the meal is rounded off with a special *aarti* (blessing) of the children. They are also given *channa* (Bengal gram) and milk as *prasad*.

All through *Shravan*, mothers observe a special fast on Friday praying to a different *Jivti* (a heavenly spirit, like a fairy Godmother) each time praying for the protection of their children. This picture can be bought at any grocery store selling typically Maharashtrian goods.

Bhadrapad (Mid August-Mid September)

HARITAALIKA

This all-women festival is actually a fast undertaken to ensure the long life of one's husband. Celebrated the day before the Ganesh idol is brought in to the home, it is a day of fasting and prayer. There is a story behind it: even though her father, Himalaya, had promised her hand to Lord Vishnu, Parvati had set her heart on marrying Lord Shiva. So she ran away from home and hid in the forest with the help of a friend. There, all night long Parvati prayed to a *Shivling* (representation of Shiva) fashioned from sand, invoking his help and intervention. This deep devotion disturbed Shiva's penance and he appeared before her promising to grant her every wish. She asked for only one - that he marry her. So the next morning Parvati immersed the Shivling in the river, happy that she had got her way. When the desperate father finally found his daughter he consented to the marriage of Parvati and Shiva. Thus a triumphant Parvati returned home and was married to Shiva in a grand celebration. It is to honour this day that women observe a fast and pray to get the same husband in their next lives (which according to my father is an insurance policy for at least some husbands!), while young girls pray for a good husband in this life. The festival is celebrated with a fast of either fruit or fasting food. This festival also heralds the festival of *Ganesh Chaturthi*.

GANESH CHATURTHI

This beloved God of Maharashtra is welcomed each year for a ten-day stay. Amid much fanfare, he is installed in a special place in the home, lovingly decorated and venerated with an *aarti*, morning and evening. With everybody singing hymns with great passion, marking the beat by ringing bells, clanging cymbals (*zhanza*), or just loud clapping, this becomes quite a noisy celebration! Some families have a traditional Ganesh and they have a custom-made idol in exactly the same form year after year. This *poojecha* Ganpati is a very solemn affair and the custom of worshipping it is carried down through the generations. At such a celebration, all the members of the family attend the *pooja*, which is strictly followed with no deviation or shortcuts. However, many families, like ours for instance, bring home a small Ganesha just for the thrill of it. Lord Ganesh comes to our homes from *Ganesh Chaturthi* to *Anant Chaturdashi*, a period of 10 days. In most families, the Ganesh idol is kept only for a day and a half, though some people keep him home for 5 days, 7 and even all 10 days. Though this festival has now generated a lot of noise, thanks to the loud music blaring in *Sarvajanik Ganeshotsavs*, and the very eco-unfriendly way of making and immersing of the idols, it still remains a well-loved festival. Apart from meeting one's friends, one looks forward to the special *prasad of modak* that Ganpati is so fond of. Note that as *modak* is the food for a god, jaggery is used and not sugar.

Modak

SWEET COCONUT DUMPLINGS

Ingredients

1 teaspoon ghee (*toop*)
1 cup rice flour
1 cup grated coconut
¾ cup grated jaggery
A pinch of saffron threads
A pinch of cardamom powder

Method

- Bring 1 cup of water to a boil in a pan.
- When the water starts bubbling add the ghee and rice flour and stir briskly till it becomes a thick paste and take off the heat. Cover tightly, and set aside to cool.
- To make the stuffing, place the coconut, jaggery, saffron and cardamom powder in a pan and cook till the jaggery melts.
- Knead the dough and divide into 3-4 balls.
- Grease your palms and shape the dough into small cups and stuff them with the coconut mixture. Pinch the edges of the pastry to make well-defined ridges or pleats. Gather the edges together on top and seal them together forming a peak.
- Place the modak in a steamer lined with a large damp piece of muslin, making sure the muslin covers the *modak* as well, and steam for 10 minutes.
- Serve hot with ghee.

RISHIPANCHAMI

The second day of the Ganesh festival is celebrated as *Rishipanchami*, a two-tier festival that acknowledges the labour of the oxen that make it possible for us to eat all year round, and also honours the sages who made our lives possible.

Since the food we eat every day is thanks to the labour of the oxen used to till the soil, the beasts of burden are given the day off and we only eat vegetables and food that grow without the help of animals. Traditionally, on this particular day, the women of the house collect all the possible vegetables and roots that are not 'cultivated' and put them in a huge pot to cook gently in their own juices for at least four hours. Apart from the greens, you should also add bits of corn (but I wonder how this qualifies to be an uncultivated vegetable).

However, if you really want to cook the dish, go to any market in the Konkan or Mumbai area on the day of the festival, or even a day before, and ask for '*rishichi bhaaji*' and the *bhaajiwalla* (vegetable vendor) will oblige with a basket of five to twenty-one different leafy vegetables used to make this dish.

The sages Kashyap, Bharadwaj, Vishwamitra, Gautam, Jamdagni, Atri, Vashisht and his wife Arundhati are also remembered on this day and thanked for their selfless dedication and devotion. Women observe a fast on this day and ask for forgiveness for any sins committed, knowingly or unknowingly.

GAURI POOJA

On the fourth day Gauri, mother of Ganpati is welcomed. On the fifth day after Ganpati is enthroned in the house, Ganpati and his mother Gauri are worshipped. Traditionally a ladies' lunch is organised at which the special dish Ghavan (page 177) and Ghatla (page 178) is served. The ladies who are invited are welcomed with the ritual *haldi-kunku*. In the evening, Gauri and the Ganpati who have been worshipped in the home for 5 days, are immersed. Gauri is brought home in the form of five smooth dark pebbles and placed alongside the Ganpati idol. Doodh Gool Shevaiya (page 179) can also be served on this day.

Ghavan

CUCUMBER PANCAKES

Akin to the better-known *dosa*, this rice pancake is made mainly by *Kokanasthas*, particularly on this day as it is considered to be the Goddess Gauri's favourite dish. Unlike the *dosa*, though, this does not require any fermentation and can be made as a quick snack at any other time as well.

Ingredients

2 cups grated cucumber
2 cups sugar or jaggery
1 cup rice flour
3 cups wholewheat flour
Salt to taste
Oil for shallow-frying

Method

- Place the grated cucumber in a pan. Add the sugar and cook for 5 minutes.
- Add the rice flour, mix well and take off the heat. Cool.
- Add the wholewheat flour and salt and mix well to make a thick batter. If the batter is too thick, add some water to adjust the consistency.
- Heat a *tawa* and drizzle a little oil over it. Pour a tablespoonful of batter and spread it in a circular motion into a thin disc. Cook on one side. Then flip over and cook the other side.
- Serve this spongy pancake with *Ghatla* (recipe follows).

Note: can also be made without the cucumber, or with grated pumpkin instead of cucumber.

Ghatla

COCONUT SAUCE

This delicately flavoured coconut sauce or gravy is the perfect and traditional accompaniment to *ghavan*.

Ingredients

1 cup grated fresh coconut

½ cup sugar or grated jaggery, or to taste

½ teaspoon cardamom powder

Method

- To extract coconut milk, grind the grated coconut. Place in a piece of muslin and squeeze out the milk.
- Add the jaggery and cardamom powder.
- Bring to a gentle simmer.
- Serve cold with Ghavan (page 177).

Note: To prevent the coconut milk from curdling, add 1 teaspoon rice flour and whisk to avoid lumps from forming.

Doodh Gool Shevaiya

DOUBLE COOKED RICE NOODLES WITH SWEET JAGGERY SAUCE

Ingredients

11 teaspoon ghee (*toop*)
1 cup rice flour
1 cup milk
¼ teaspoon cardamom powder
¼ cup jaggery
1-2 saffron threads

Method

- Bring 1 cup of water to a boil in a pan with ghee. Then quickly add the rice flour. Stir briskly; turn off the heat and cover allowing it to cool in a covered pan.
- When cool, knead well.
- Make into smooth balls and again drop them into boiling water.
- When double cooked, press through a *shev*-press to make noodles.
- Make a sweet sauce with milk, cardamom, jaggery and saffron threads.
- Serve the coconut sauce with noodles.

ANANTH CHATURDASHI

After ten days of being feted, Lord Ganesh is given a fond farewell by his devotees. Since all idols have to be immersed, they are generally carried to a nearby water body like a river, lake or sea. In today's day and age, song and dance and wild street processions mark the deities' journey from the *pandals* to the sea or river, and sadly this festival today has metamorphosed into the idiom of our times far removed from the quiet homely celebration that served to bring families and communities together. However, with modern day sensibilities of protecting the environment, several families have resorted to praying to a metallic idol in silver, brass or copper and immersing it in a bucket of water before putting it away till the following year. Supposedly, the idol gets 'energised' when it is prayed to, and this energy should be neutralised before being stored away, hence the immersion in a bucket of water is absolutely essential.

To celebrate the immersion, Sanzachya Polya (page 139) are traditionally cooked on this day.

PITRUPAKSH

Perhaps it is only natural that after 14 days of hectic celebration, the body should be given a rest, and the spirit begins to seek the blessings of one's ancestors. According to an aunt of mine, it is only when we remember our departed ancestors do we also realise the importance of not getting attached to worldly goods.

So, in pursuit of this higher spiritual level, the latter half of Bhadrapada month is dedicated to the worship and remembrance of the family members who have passed away. Hence this period is considered to be inauspicious and people avoid starting new ventures or indulging in major purchases. Certain days in this period are dedicated to a specific ancestor.

Bharni Shraadh on the fourth day is dedicated to all those who passed away in the current year. In the first year of a person's death his soul resides in *Pitruloka*, a place between heaven and earth. Hence this ceremony can only be performed by an outsider like a priest, and not by a member of the bereaved family.

Avidhva Navmi or the ninth day is dedicated to the memory of all female ancestors who died as married women or *savashin*. As part of the celebrations for this day, a meal is offered to a *savashin*.

Dwadashi Shraadh or the twelfth day commemorates all those souls who became sanyasis or renunciants.

Chaturdhashi Shraadh or the fourteenth day, is dedicated to the memory of those ancestors who were killed, murdered or who died in accidents.

Sarvapitri Amavas on the fifteenth and last day is dedicated to all ancestors.

It is only after the first year of a person's death that his soul is welcomed to the nether world by the souls of his forefathers when the *Varsha Shraadh* is performed. After this first year when *Shraadh* can only be performed by a priest, all subsequent *Shraadhs* for that person can be performed by any family member.

Ashvin (Mid September–Mid October)

NAVRATRI – THE FESTIVAL OF NINE NIGHTS

Navratri is another of those festivals that is celebrated in different ways by different families. Some place a lighted lamp before the family *devghar* for 24 hours for all 9 days. Some observe *Navratri* by placing a special garland of marigolds on the family shrine, adding a new one each day and removing all nine on Dussera, replacing the 9 garlands with a special garland on Vijayadashmi. During these nine days there are cultural programmes, *pooja*, *homs* and *havans*.

The Mother Goddess is worshipped in her three different forms.

Days 1-3	Mahashakti - courage and strength
Days 4-6	Mahalakshmi - Wealth and prosperity
Days 7-9	Mahasaraswati - Knowledge and learning

This nine-day festival is celebrated by the Kokanasthas with the *Bondla* or special get-together for young girls. Usually held by turns in neighbourhood homes, young girls gather at around sunset around the *tulsi vrindavan* in the courtyard. The rest of the evening is spent around an elephant *rangoli* - dancing, singing folk songs and playing traditional games like *phugadi* and *kombdi*.

Phugadi is a dance where the girls dance in pairs, holding hands with arms outstretched and crossed in front with feet close and touching so that their bodies are at an angle. Thus positioned, whirl round and round till the last pair remains standing with the rest falling off dizzy by the way.

Kombdi is a game where the girls move around on their haunches, flap their arms bent at the elbow and squawk like hens. Once again the girl that outlasts the others is considered the winner. Generally on the first day, one song is sung while on the second two, and so on and so forth. The highlight of these celebrations is the goody bag or food that each girl brings to the celebrations, as well as the goodies they take back home. All the little girls are expected to guess what the *khirapat* (yummies in the goody bag) are: usually treats like *laadoo* or dried fruit and nuts.

Like most other traditions, this one too is dying out, especially when *Kokanasthas* live in far-away places. In my entire lifetime, I have only attended one *Bondla*, while my daughters are completely oblivious of such a custom!

LALITA PANCHAMI

On the fifth day of *Navratri*, 48 bundles of *durva*, (which is a stalk of grass with 3,5, or 11 blades), each one of which is made up of 48 *durva*, are offered to the Goddess Lalita (the Divine Goddess or Parvati) along with a heartfelt prayer for her blessings of knowledge, wealth and prosperity.

VIJAYA DASHMI OR DUSSERA

The harvest festival, Dussera, universally celebrated by Hindus all over India, is marked by Maharashtrians and *Kokanasthas* with an exchange of *sona* or cassia leaves between the elders of the family and the youngsters who come to greet them. This is considered as one of the 3½ auspicious days which do not require an astrological validation to start anything new. Hence a number of new ventures are begun on this day.

Traditionally, this would be the first day for a young child to enter school and he would begin his school year by drawing the symbol of Saraswati on his slate, offering her flowers and *kunku*, seeking her blessings as he starts this new phase of his life. In the evening, the children go to the edges of the village to locate a cassia tree, perform a *pooja* and bring home the leaves as 'gold' which they offer to their elders as they bow to seek their blessings. The ladies of the house then do a special *ovalni* of the children and offer them *sona* as a gift. The special sweet on Dussera is either Shrikhand (page 183) or Baasundi (page 156).

There are so many reasons to celebrate Dussera: it commemorates the day when Kuber (Treasurer of the Heavens) on King Raghuraj's entreaty rained gold coins on Ayodhya. Dussera also marks the return of the Pandavas from their exile in the forest, a day when they took up arms once again to continue their fight against the Kauravas, as recounted in the Mahabharata. So on this day, soldiers and craftsmen worship the tools of their trade. And finally, this is the day when the Mother Goddess Durga destroyed the Demon Mahishasura.

Shrikhand

SAFFRON-FLAVOURED YOGHURT

Ingredients

2 litres milk
1 tablespoon yoghurt
1½ cups finely powdered sugar
1 teaspoon cardamom powder
¼ teaspoon nutmeg powder
4-5 saffron threads
1 teaspoon milk
A pinch of salt

Method

- Heat the milk in a pan till warm to touch.
- Line the insides of a bowl with yoghurt and add the warm milk. This will ensure that the yoghurt will be thick and creamy. Place in a warm, place for 8 hours to set.
- Place the set yoghurt in a piece of muslin, tie it up in a bundle (*potli*), and hang to drain, for 2 hours.
- Place the drained yoghurt in a bowl and add the powdered sugar. Set aside to rest for 30 minutes.
- Spread the piece of muslin tightly over a deep bowl and use as a sieve.
- Rub the yoghurt with your fingers through the sieve to get a smooth paste. You could also do this by blending the mixture in a blender in brief spurts, to ensure that there are no lumps. However, if processed for to long this can lead to a runny *shrikhand*,
- Add the cardamom and nutmeg powder to the paste.
- In a pan, gently heat the saffron threads, and add the milk. Crush the saffron threads with the back of a spoon to release the aroma and colour of the spice. Add a pinch of salt.
- Add to the *shrikhand*, stir to mix and serve with hot Puri (page 132).

On this particular winter night, when the moon is closest to the earth, the moonlight is particularly spectacular and while the moon is up, the Goddess Laxmi is believed to visit our homes, asking the question "Ko Jagarati?" or "Who is awake?" So everyone stays up till midnight, their houses ablaze with light to show Laxmi the way, enjoying the moonlight and sipping masala milk.

On this day it is customary for a mother to gift her first-born a special gift. A sister-in-law of mine explained the connection between this particular full moon night and a mother's love for her first born: the love of a mother for her first born is akin to the passion a full moon inspires. Thus a mother gifts her first born a white garment. My mother always gave me a special gift starting out with a white dress as a child, which evolved into a white *saree* when I grew up and occasionally became a white *salwar* suit, a white leather bag or even white shoes (gifting shoes is actually considered in poor taste as it may be construed as giving someone the boot!) as I began tiring of white *sarees.* Since only the eldest child is bestowed with these gifts, and since both my girls are so close in age, I didn't want to discriminate between them, and have never followed this custom in my own home. It is important that the gift be white because the moon is at its whitest and brightest at this time of year.

Masala Doodh

SWEET SPICED MILK

Ingredients

½ litre milk

1 cup soaked almonds, skinned and ground into a fine paste

4 teaspoons sugar

½ teaspoon powdered cardamom

2-3 saffron threads

Method

- Heat the milk in a pan. When the milk begins to boil, add the almond paste, sugar, cardamom powder and the saffron. Should you add these to the milk while cold, it will curdle.
- Cool, refrigerate and enjoy chilled.

Note: Remember to keep your windows and doors wide open for Goddess Laxmi to enter, and the house well-lit so that she does not lose her way to your home.

DIWALI

The festival of lights which is universally celebrated by all Hindus doesn't really need any introduction. Traditionally the festivities begin with *Vasubaras* celebrated on the 12th day of *Ashvin* and ends with *Bhaubeej* on the 2nd day of *Karthik*. In between we have *Dhantrayodashi* the day on which we can officially start putting up the lights, *Narakchaturdashi*, the day of the traditional early morning oil bath, *amavas* (the dark moonless night) or *Lakshmi poojan*, and *Padva* or New Year.

VASUBARAS

A throwback to the days when ours was an agrarian society and wealth was measured in land and heads of cattle, *Vasubaras* is a day dedicated to the cow and her calf. It is said that 33 crore gods reside in the cow and worshipping her is equivalent to worshipping 33 crore gods! The milch cow also symbolises motherhood which is another reason to worship her.

DHANTRAYODASHI

There are two stories associated with *Dhantrayodashi* which is celebrated the day after *Vasubaras*. According to one story, there was once a king in ancient India called Hemdev. The king had a son who got married and being a prince, had a grand princely wedding. However, tragedy struck within 4 days of the wedding and the prince was pronounced dead. Obviously the young bride was desolate and clung on desperately to the prince's body. Seeing her grief, the messenger of Yama, the God of death, who had come to collect the body, couldn't bring himself to tear away the desolate young widow clutching onto her dear husband and he returned to Yama empty-handed. On witnessing this, Yama agreed to stave off an early death if people observed a five day festival of lights from that day on. This is why *Dhantryodashi* began to be celebrated.

In yet another story, this is the day to honour *Dhanwantri*, physician to the gods, seek his blessings for good health particularly before the festival of Diwali. To celebrate, place a lamp facing the South, worship some coins and distribute a *prasad* of *bataasa* and puffed wheat (*lhaaya*).

NARAKCHATURDASHI

The 14th day of *Ashvin* commemorates the slaying of the demon Narkasur by Lord Shri Krishna. It is said that Narkasur was the demon who abducted young virgins from other lands and imprisoned them in his kingdom. With the help of his wife Satyabhama, Lord Shri Krishna attacked and killed the demon and freed the young girls. So on this day, people awake before daybreak, have a scented bath and put on all the lights to signify the breaking of a new dawn. It is said that he who fails to follow the ritual early morning bath on this day is destined to perish in hell.

The darkest night of *Ashvin* is celebrated as *Laxmi poojan* when the Goddess of Wealth is supposed to visit one's home. Once again, she is welcomed with a clean home and bright lights.

Karthik (Mid October-Mid November)

The first day of Karthik is celebrated as Balipratipada or the day when King Bali a staunch enemy of the Gods, was destroyed by Vaman (Vishnu in the form of a dwarf). The story goes that Lord Vishnu as Vaman, went up to King Bali and asked him for a gift of land that could be covered in three strides. Observing his short stature, the king readily agreed and was shocked when Vaman claimed the whole earth and the sky with the first two steps! Before he knew it, Vaman placed the third step on King Bali's head and thus Vaman banished the wicked king to the underworld. However, Vishnu was impressed with Bali's generosity and rewarded him by appointing him as King and Gatekeeper of the Netherworld. I don't know what the connection is between King Bali and this *Padva* because it is also a special day for husbands. On this day, traditionally, the wife gives her husband a good oil massage, a hot bath and also performs an *ovalni* making sure he gets all his favourite food. Naturally, he rewards her devotion with an appropriate gift of a *saree*, ornaments or cash.

Sometimes *Padva* is in the morning while *Bhaubeej* is in the evening which means that the *ovalni* of the husband has to be done well in time, lest you land up performing *ovalni* for a brother!

Days 1	*Vasubaras*
Days 2	*Dhantrayodashi*
Days 3	*Narak Chaturdashi*
Days 4	*Amavas or Laxmi Poojan*
Days 5	*Balipratipada*
Days 6	*Bhaubeej*

PHARAAL OR DIWALI SWEETS

The major grouse of all the *ajjis* today is that *pharaal* is no longer restricted to Diwali. Thanks to all the shops selling ready-to-eat goodies all year round, *laadoo* and *chaklis* have lost the glamour associated with Diwali. However, Diwali is not Diwali without at least some *pharaal* or special Diwali treats, served and eaten on the morning of Diwali. Traditional Diwali *pharaal* include sweet and savoury delights like Karanji (Page 187), Ravyache Laadoo (page 188), Chirote (page 191), Chakli (page 192) and an unusual sweet called Anarse (page 200).

Karanji

COCONUT TURNOVERS

This yummy coconut-stuffed pastry is easy to make ahead of time. Stored in an airtight container they stay well for about a week (if they last that long).

Ingredients

Pastry

¾ cup refined flour (*maida*)
1 tablespoon ghee (*toop*) + for deep-frying
A pinch of salt
Milk for greasing

Stuffing

1 cup freshly grated coconut
½ teaspoon cardamom powder
¾ cup sugar
2-3 saffron threads
1 tablespoon almond slivers

Method

- Mix together all the ingredients for the stuffing and set aside till the sugar dissolves.
- If the sugar has not dissolved completely, gently heat the mixture till the sugar melts, making sure it does not discolour.
- Mix the ingredients for the pastry, adding a little water, and knead to make a firm dough. Divide the dough into 8 equal portions and roll into discs. Place a tablespoon of stuffing on one half of the disc. Brush the edge of the other half with some milk and gently fold over and seal to make a semi-circle. Trim the edge with a pastry cutter.
- Heat the ghee in a *kadai* and deep-fry the *karanji* on low heat till golden.
- Drain on absorbent paper and store in an air-tight jar.

Makes 8-10 medium karanji

Note: The *karanji* should be crisp and stored in an air-tight tin. Since the coconut is fresh, if you intend keeping it for a long time, they should be stored in a refrigerator.

Ravyache Laadoo

SWEET SEMOLINA BALLS

Though this is a staple at *Diwali* and other occasions like weddings, it is a special favourite with my children and me, and we often make it during the year. It is also very convenient to have around the house when you are flooded with guests, especially little ones who can happily help themselves to a *laadoo* or two, stored in a steel *dabba* (container).

Ingredients

1 tablespoon ghee (*toop*)
2 cups semolina, sifted
1 cup freshly grated coconut
A pinch of saffron threads
1 teaspoon cardamom powder
6-7 almonds, soaked, peeled and slivered
2 tablespoons raisins
1 tablespoon milk
1 cup sugar

Method

- Heat the ghee in a *kadai* or large flat-bottomed pan, and roast the semolina till it turns brown and fragrant.
- Add the coconut and roast for a few minutes. Add the saffron, cardamom powder, almond slivers, and raisins.
- Stir well and pour into a *paraat* or a large shallow dish. Sprinkle milk over the mixture and stir well.
- In a pan mix together the sugar and ¾ cup water and heat to make a sticky syrup. Remember to test the syrup from time to time because if the syrup gets too concentrated, the resulting *laadoo* can become embarrassingly hard and difficult to bite into. Of course if you like them hard then go ahead and make a syrup of one-thread consistency.
- Add the syrup to the semolina mixture and mix well.
- Shape the mixture into 22-24 small balls, or 10-12 large balls.
- Store in an air-tight container.

Makes 24 laadoo

Note: The trick to the syrup is actually closely observing the changes in its consistency. To begin with the syrup is milky and rather murky looking but once the sugar begins to crystallise it turns startlingly clear. That's when you should test for stickiness and then quickly stir in the semolina mixture.

Besanache Laadoo

SWEET GRAM FLOUR BALLS

Ingredients

2 tablespoons ghee (*toop*)
1 cup gram flour
¼ cup milk
1 cup powdered sugar
½ teaspoon cardamom powder
6-7 almonds, soaked, peeled and slivered
3-4 saffron threads

Method

- Heat the ghee in a *kadai* and add the gram flour and roast on low heat, stirring continuously, till fragrant. Remove from heat.
- Sprinkle the milk to make the mixture fluffy.
- Add the powdered sugar, cardamom powder, almond slivers and saffron, and mix well. Leave to cool.
- Once the mixture has cooled completely, shape into small balls.
- Store in an air-tight container.

Note: These *laadoo* are extremely healthy and are handy while travelling.

Chivda

CRISP SPICY RICE FLAKES

Almost every home has *chivda* at all times of the year, though at *Diwali* it is particularly welcome to counteract the overdose of sweetness around. There are two ways of making *chivda* – one is to deep-fry it and the other one with a seasoning added. *Chivda* can also be made out of *pohe*, *kurmure*, potatoes, and nowadays, even corn flakes! However, traditionally for *Diwali* there is only the one *chivda* and this is made out of *pohe*.

Ingredients

½ kg thick beaten rice (*jade pohe*)
½ dried coconut, slivered
150 grams roasted split Bengal gram (*daali*)
150 grams cashew nuts
150 grams peanuts
150 grams almonds
150 grams raisins
Salt to taste
½ teaspoon sugar
Oil for deep-frying

Seasoning

1 teaspoon oil
1 teaspoon mustard seeds
½ teaspoon turmeric powder
5-6 curry leaves
4-5 green chillies, cut into half

Method

- Heat the oil in a *kadai* and deep-fry all the ingredients separately. Drain on absorbent paper.
- For the seasoning, heat the oil in a *kadai*, and add the mustard seeds. Then add turmeric powder, curry leaves and green chillies and take off the heat.
- Mix together all the ingredients adding seasoning. Add salt and sugar.
- Cool and store in an air-tight container.

Chirote

SWEET LAYERED PASTRY

Delicate, sugared puff pastry. That is about the best description of this light and unusual *Diwali* sweet. Actually making it is far easier than one would imagine.

Ingredients

1 cup refined flour (*maida*)
1 tablespoon hot ghee (*toop*)
+ 2 cups ghee (*toop*) for deep-frying
½ cup powdered sugar for dusting
A pinch of salt

Shortening

1 teaspoon ghee (*toop*)
1 tablespoon rice flour

Method

- Sift the flour in a *paarat* or mixing bowl.
- Add a pinch of salt and 1 tablespoon hot ghee, and mix well with a spoon, till it resembles breadcrumbs.
- Add a little water and knead lightly to make a dough. Do not overwork the dough or the pastry will lose its lightness.
- Set aside, covered, to prevent the dough from drying out, for 1-2 hours.
- For the shortening, whisk together, the ghee and rice flour with your fingers to make a smooth but frothy paste. Divide the dough into 4-5 equal balls and roll them out into thin discs (*poli*).
- Dot each *poli* with the shortening and roll them up tightly, like a Swiss roll.
- Cut each roll into equal pieces.
- Gently roll out the pieces into ¼-inch thick ovals.
- Heat the ghee in a *kadai* and deep-fry the *chirote* on low heat, ladling the hot ghee over them to ensure they are evenly cooked. When the ghee stops sizzling, the chirote are done. Drain on absorbent paper and cool.
- Dust the cooled *chirote* with powdered sugar.
- Alternatively, *chirote* can be dipped in dipped in sugar syrup.

Chakli

SPICY DEEP-FRIED SPIRALS

Traditionally *chakli* are made out of a mixture of various ingredients. Weeks before they are to be made, these grains are washed, dried and roasted in a *kadai* and ground into *bhaajni* or roasted flour. The exact proportion of the rice, *dal* and dried coriander seeds is normally a family secret and varies from family to family.

Ingredients

3 cups Bhaajni Flour (recipe below)
Salt to taste
½ teaspoon turmeric powder
½ teaspoon chilli powder
½ teaspoon white sesame seeds
2½ tablespoons hot oil +
2 cups oil for deep-frying

Method

- Mix together the flour, salt, turmeric powder, chilli powder, sesame seeds and hot oil (*mohun*) and knead to make a stiff dough.
- Tightly pack the dough into a *chakli* press and pipe out the *chakli* into a spiral of tight concentric circles on a sheet of greaseproof paper.
- Heat the oil in a *kadai*. Slide the *chakli* in gently one by one, and lower the heat to allow for even cooking.
- Once the oil stops sizzling, and the *chakli* sink to the bottom, they are done. Remove with a slotted spoon, drain on absorbent paper and cool.
- Store the *chakli* in an air-tight container.

Note: You can increase the quantity of chilli powder if you prefer spicier *chakli*.

Bhaajni

MULTI-GRAIN FLOUR

Ingredients

3 cups rice
1 cup split Bengal gram (*chana dal*)
1 cup split green gram (*moong dal*)
1 cup split black gram (*urad dal*)
½ cup dried coriander seeds
¼ cup cumin seeds

Method

- Wash and dry the rice and *dal*, separately.
- Heat a *tawa* and dry-roast the *dal*, separately.
- Dry-roast separately, the coriander seeds and cumin seeds.
- Mix together all the roasted ingredients and grind into a fine flour.

BHAUBEEJ

This festival commemorates the great love and devotion between the hard-hearted Yama and his sister Yami. Like *Padva, Bhaubeej* is marked with an early morning bath where the sister gives the brother an oil massage followed by a warm, scented bath. Naturally, this is only done in childhood. Then she honours him with *aukshan* or *aarti* which he reciprocates with an *ovalni* (gift of cash or kind). Generally the brother is invited to his sister's house on that day and she cooks him all his favourite foods.

KARTIKI EKADASHI

Lord Vishnu, the protector of the Earth who goes to sleep on *Ashadhi Ekadashi*, wakes up on this day and the four-month period of *Chaturmas* officially comes to an end. Thus people keep a fast on this day and pray to Lord Vithal or Pandurang, the deity symbolising the union of the three gods of our trinity Brahma, Vishnu and Shiva.

TULSICHA LAGNA

The twelfth day of *Karthik* is celebrated as the wedding of Lord Vishnu and the humble Tulsi who was actually the wife of a demon called Jalandhar. It is said that due to the devotion and piety of his pure and chaste wife Vrinda, the demon Jalandar had become so powerful that he was a threat to the gods. Jalandhar had also been promised that as long as his wife was true and faithful to him, he could not be killed. So in order to kill him, Lord Vishnu disguised himself as Jalandhar and seduced the unsuspecting Vrinda. When Vrinda discovered Vishnu's treachery, she cursed him and transformed him into a stone and herself into a tulsi (holy *basil*) plant. But Lord Vishnu was so in love with her that he restored her honour by marrying her even as a *tulsi* plant.

This day also marks the beginning of the availability of seasonal fruits like tamarind, Indian gooseberry (*awla*), wood apple (*kavat*), Indian jujube (*bor*) the natural sources of Vitamin C that help keep infections at bay.

VAIKUNTHA CHATURDASHI

This marks the day when Lord Vishnu decided to worship Lord Shiva with 1000 pure white lotuses. At the last moment, Lord Vishnu couldn't find the last flower because Lord Shiva had hidden it to test his devotion. Undaunted, Lord Vishnu took out one of his eyes and offered that instead. Seeing this extreme dedication, Lord Shiva was so pleased that he gave him the *Sudarshan Chakra* with the blessing that with it he could overpower any evil force. Thus on this day, people observe a fast, pray to Lord Vishnu in the night and to Lord Shiva at daybreak, offering a white lotus to each of them.

TRIPURI POORNIMA

The lights lit on this full moon night signify the illumination of good thoughts within a person.

Marghasheesh (Mid Nov-Mid December)

DATTA JAYANTI

The major festival in this month is the birth anniversary of the three-headed God Dattatreya, a God worshipped largely in Maharasthra. This God who is the synthesis of the Hindu trinity Brahma, Vishnu and Shiva, has a very interesting tale associated with his creation. Apparently the trinity of gods was so intrigued by the chastity of Anusuya, the beautiful wife of the sage Atreya that they wanted to test her loyalty. So with the intention of seducing her, the three of them stealthily hid behind the bushes, while she was bathing by the river. However, Anusaya sensed that she was not alone and willed who ever it was spying on her to change into the form of innocent babes, thereby ensuring that her nakedness was only seen through the eyes of innocence. Thus her chastity remained intact. The gods were not only impressed by her fidelity, but also ashamed of their behaviour, and asking her forgiveness promised to grant her a wish. The childless Anusuya asked that the three gods be born to her as a child, and this is how Dattatreya, the three-headed God came into this world.

Paush (Mid December-Mid January)

The month of Paush is the coldest month of the year and the dry cold weather brings with it its own special treats. This is the season when sugar cane is harvested. You can often spot smoke curling from a sugar cane farm where the cane juice is brought to a thick bubbly mass in a large open air *kadai*. This is the season for making unrefined sugar that is healthy and wholesome. It is also harvest time for sesame seeds, *bajra* or millet, so it is but natural that festival of *Bhogi*, which is celebrated the day before *Makarsankranti* is a time where Bajri Bhaakri (page 133) sprinkled with sesame seeds, Masaale Khichadi (page 37) and *dahi* are the order of the day. Some families also take this opportunity to make a mixed *bhaaji* of *papdi* (broad beans), carrots, brinjal, *pavte* (Lima beans) and *methi* (fenugreek leaves).

The day after this festival, which interestingly falls on 14th January every year, is *Makarsankranti*, which marks the ascent of the sun into the northern hemisphere. This occasion is normally celebrated with the distribution of *halwa* or sweets made of sesame seeds. My father-in-law, who grew up in the Vidharbha region, remembers distributing small earthen pots filled with pieces of fresh sugar cane, carrots and Indian gooseberries to his friends on this day.

As with most festivals, there is a story behind the celebration. Sankrant commemorates the slaying of the two warring demons, Sankasur (on Makarsankrant) and Kankasur (the following day) by one ugly and arrogant Goddess, who earned the name *Sankranti* after killing Sankasur. This is also the day we request our neighbours and friends to let bygones be bygones, and ask for forgiveness for any hurt or misunderstanding that may have been caused, either knowingly or unknowingly, and present them with a gift of *teelache laadoo* or *halwa* saying, "*Tilgool ghya, god god bola*" which translates as, "May you talk sweetly to me with this sweet offering of mine".

The first *Sankrant* after her wedding is an important event for a bride, and she is made to feel special with a gift of a black *saree* embroidered with white star motifs. Her mother-in-law also honours her by hosting a special *haldi-kunku*. The young bride is bedecked in special handmade ornaments made out of *halwa* (small sesame candy). Apart from the Teelache Laadoo (page 196) given to the ladies for the *haldi-kunku*, the special 'goodie bag' has assorted berries like Indian gooseberries, pieces of sugarcane and peanuts. Along with the traditional celebratory meal, the specialty of the day is the Gool Poli (page 138).

Teelache Laadoo

SWEET SESAME SEED BALLS

These are my all-time favourite *laadoo*, and even though I make them all year round, I believe they taste particularly delicious at this time of year.

Ingredients

500 grams white polished sesame seeds
125 grams coarsely ground roasted peanuts
120 grams grated dried coconut
300 grams jaggery

Method

- Dry-roast the sesame seeds in a *kadai* stirring all the time to ensure even roasting.
- Remove from heat and stir in the peanut powder and grated coconut.
- Melt the jaggery in a double boiler stirring all the time and taking care that it does not get too dark and over caramelised. When the jaggery is ready to use it aquires a glossy sheen and begins to bubble. To test for doneness, drop a tiny dollop into a bowl of cold water. It should immediately form a soft ball. If you like your *laadoo* 'break-your-teeth' hard, cook the jaggery for just a little bit longer.
- Add the dry ingredients to the melted jaggery and stir well to mix. Allow to cool a little before shaping into laadoo or bite-sized balls with well-greased hands. The mark of a good *laadoo* is that it should resonate sharply when placed on a stainless steel plate!

Makes 80 small laadoo

Note: These *laadoo* are best made with *chikkicha gool*, a type of jaggery which sets really hard when cool. Unfortunately, it is not very easy to come by, so you may have to vary the quantity of jaggery so that the *laadoo* bind well together.

Magh (Mid January-Mid February)

GANESH JAYANTI

The fourth day of this month is the birthday of Lord Ganesh. Everyone knows that Parvati made Ganesh from the dirt she rubbed out of her body. She often asked her son to keep watch outside the bathroom while she was bathing. When her Lord and Master, Shiva came home to find this young guard stop him from entering the bathroom, he angrily chopped his head off. It was only when Parvati told him that Ganesh was her own child that he realised that he had beheaded his own son! The repentant husband ran out of the house determined to transfer the head of the first living creature he found and fix it on the headless Ganesh. It so happened that the first being he espied was an elephant and that is how Ganesh came to have an elephant's head. However, the festival of Ganesh is celebrated in the month of *Bhadrapad* (August- September).

VASANT PANCHAMI

With the weather still pleasant and just about getting warmer, this fifth day of Magh is celebrated as the official beginning of spring but is not celebrated in any special way.

MAHASHIVRATRI

The fourteenth day of the dark half of this month is celebrated as the festival of Shiva.

An uncle-in-law who regularly does the *Laghurudra pooja* in our family tells me that Shiva is one of those Gods who likes to live rough. Not for him the lavish palaces or thrones lined with cushions: the cremation ground is where you are most likely to find him with matted hair and a fierce expression on his face. The festival of Shiva is celebrated with austerity – by fasting. The only difference being that this fast is observed while eschewing *varyache tandool* and Daanyachi Aamti (page 165), since these were the two foods that Shiva particularly disliked! Devotees of Shiva are so wary of displeasing this God who demands strict allegiance, that they observe the fast for both meals.

Phalgun (Mid February-Mid March)

HOLI

As little kids growing up in Pune, we used to recite an obscene rhyme venerating Holi and the *puran poli* while mocking the Englishmen who had ruled us all those years ago. I have, of course, not experienced colonial rule, but this ditty must have been one of those childhood chants that are passed on from one generation to the next, because it is still recited by young children.

Puran Poli (page 136) is, according to my mother, the ultimate test of a good cook. She also claims it was a special device to keep the woman chained to the stove, while the menfolk went out to have a good time.

Holi, as it was traditionally celebrated, consisted of a bonfire celebrating the victory of Good over Evil. Then five days later was the Spring festival of Dhulwad, where powdered colour (particularly red gulal) was playfully smeared on all the participants.

Today, this festival has been condensed to just one day - Holi - and has metamorphosed into a pan-Indian celebration of wet colour - even oil paint - and a loutishness not seen before. But tradition dictates that this festival is marked with Puran Poli (page 136), Katachi Aamti (page 58) and Batatyachi Bhaji (page 143). Making the perfect *puran poli* really requires a lot of practice and very few cooks can get it right the first time.

The festival of Holi is actually the last festival of the year and it seems only fitting that the last full moon night of the year is spent revelling around a bonfire.

THE EXTRA MONTH

Much like the leap year in the Julian calendar, in which February has 29 days once every four years to make up the shortfall of days, the *Adhik Mahina* or *Purshottam Mahina* makes up the shortfall. Because we follow both the lunar and solar calendars, our shortfall occurs once every three years in the lunar calendar, thus depending on when it falls after the 3-year cycle, you get an *Adhik Mahina* with the name of the month that precedes it. Thus, you can have an *Adhik Shravan* or an *Adhik Chaitra*.

Each month of the year is dedicated to one of the gods in our pantheon. However, the extra month being unaccounted for, was not dedicated to any god. Totally miffed at this, the extra month complained to Lord Indra about this lapse. He also pointed out his importance in the scheme of things that he was necessary to ensure that there was no loss of time!

Appreciating this argument Indra assured him that he would be called *Purshottam mahina* and would be honoured by a unique fast. So, this month is honoured as a special month. Amongst the *Kokanasthas*, this month is particularly honoured by the lady of the house, who keeps a fast for the month and ends it by honouring 30 + 3 (not 33 mind you!) married women with the traditional *vaan* or offering which consists of a coconut, *paan supari, haldi-kunku*, a sweet, a gift either in cash or kind, and a special sweet on the last day of the month.

This special sweet should have a spongy appearance, hence the preferred sweet is the *Anarse* or Mysore *paak*. It is also customary to gift 30+3 *anarse* with a lamp to the new son-in-law for the first *Adhik Mahina* you share with him. This is supposed to multiply your blessings!

Anarse

SWEET DEEP-FRIED RICE AND POPPY SEED PASTRY

The doughnut like confection is sponge-like in appearance and dotted with poppy seeds. This unusual sweet has fallen into disfavour: perhaps it has something to do with the skill required to make the perfect *anarsa* and the fact that this sweet needs at least a week's advance preparation. The most important ingredient in the dish is rice flour, which should be made of rice that is not sticky. I find that a coarse rice grain is better than the aromatic Basmati. In addition to *Adhik Mahina*, *anarse* are also made at *Diwali*. However, should you want to try making it, here's how its done.

Ingredients

1 cup rice
¼ cup grated jaggery
1-2 tablespoons poppy seeds, for sprinkling
Ghee (*toop*) for deep-frying

Method

- To make the rice flour, the rice should be soaked for 3 days, making sure that the water is changed everyday.
- On the fourth day, drain and spread the rice out on a piece of cloth and leave to dry.
- After the rice has dried completely, pound to a flour in a large mortar and pestle. (I tried making rice flour in a mixer or pulveriser, but found that anarse only worked when the rice was pounded in the good old-fashioned *khalbatta*!)
- Knead together the rice flour and grated jaggery to make a dough. Shape into small balls and leave to ferment, in a covered container or pan for 2-3 days. Keep checking daily to ensure that the dough does not spoil. If the dough does not become pliable after 2 days, place a unripe banana in the container to help soften the dough.
- After 15 days, when the dough has fermented slightly, pat the balls into patties and sprinkle with poppy seeds on one side.
- Heat the ghee in a *kadai* and gently fry the anarse on low heat, till golden brown. Drain on absorbant paper. Store in an airtight container.

Note: Be advised that this is one recipe where rice flour just does not work. Remember, 1 cup of rice yields twice the amount of flour! Ready-made anarse flour is also available at stores specialising in Maharashtrian grocery stores particularly around *Diwali* time.

RITES OF PASSAGE

As with most traditions, the rites of passage celebrated by our ancestors have given way to more globally accepted rituals like graduation ceremonies, sweet sixteen parties, bachelor parties and celebrations to mark important events in one's life. The few which are still followed by *Kokanasthas* are the *barse* (naming ceremony), *munja* (thread ceremony or initiation into the community), *lagna* (wedding) and funeral rites.

However the 16 important rites of passage that mark a person's life are:

PRE-NATAL

Garbhadhan: Is a small *pooja* performed just before conception or shortly after conception, to ensure the progeny of one's desire. None of the people I spoke to can remember this function ever taking place save my mother who tells me that as a child she once attended such a function. The couple in question was an old couple, the man in his forties and the lady in her thirties.

Punsvan: Is a small *pooja* done in the third month of pregnancy, to ensure proper foetal development and the good health of the mother.

Simantonnayana: Is a small ceremony performed in the seventh month to ensure the correct functioning of all the sensory organs of the foetus. This is one ritual which was originally meant to entertain the young mother to be and is gaining popularity of late because of its similarity to a baby shower. This is essentially a social occasion where the mother-in-law calls all the near and dear in the family, and it ends up as a send-off party before the girl goes back to her maternal home for the delivery of her child. The mother-to-be is decked up with floral ornaments, given a new *saree* and *oatee*. What I like most about it is the guessing game that is played where the mother-to-be uncovers a masculine or feminine dish (Marathi is a language where nouns can either be masculine, feminine or of neuter gender hence this sex determination test!) With friends and family around her, she is asked to lift the *puri* covering five *vati* containing food like *kheer* (female), *laadoo* (male), *burfi* (female), *sheera* (male), *jalebi* (female), *halwa* (male).

BIRTH

Jaatkarma: The first time a father sees his newborn child, he asks God's blessing for a long, happy and prosperous life. He also touches a gold coin dipped in a mixture of honey and ghee (*toop*) to the newborn's lip.

Barse: This is a very important day as the child is given a name. Girls are named on the eleventh day while boys are named on the twelfth. Infants of both sexes have their ears pierced by the goldsmith on this day. The honour of naming the child is given to the paternal aunt who whispers it in the child's ear.

Suryavalokan: The first time, three months after birth, that a child is taken out of the home, and shown to the sun.

Annaprashan: The child is fed his first solid food, usually at six or seven months. This occasion is marked by the baby's maternal uncle feeding the baby with soft rice *kheer* with a gold ring dipped in the *kheer*.

CHILDHOOD

Chudakarm: This ritual is performed when the child is 1 year old, to support the development of self-awareness and autonomy in the child.

Karnavedha: This ritual is performed when the child is three to five years old, to support the development of self-esteem and self-respect.

END OF CHILDHOOD

Upanayan(munja): Initiation into the Brahmin fold by tying the sacred thread. This ceremony signifies the official cutting of the umbilical cord. This is a celebratory occasion when the boy is taught the secret of the *Gayatri mantra* which is whispered into his ear by his father.

Veda Arambha: Performed when the child is five to seven years old, to solidify the commitment of the child to receiving a good education.

ADULTHOOD

Samavartana or Sodmunja: Performed upon the completion of studies, to welcome the young adult as a valued member of society, ready to embark on the next stage of life, known as *Grihastha* or Household Life. A Brahmin boy can only get married after he performs this ceremony and very often this ritual is incorporated in the pre-wedding ceremonies.

Vivaha: The wedding ceremony, a series of rituals to celebrate the happy union of two people. Once again this elaborate ceremony is witnessed by friends and family and is an occasion of great joy and festivity.

RETIREMENT

Vaanaprastha Ashram: After a hard life of work, everybody likes to retire and this official rite of retirement marks the completion of the duties of household life and the entry into a new phase of life one that involves reflection and meditation.

Sanyaasa Ashram: Undertaken either after the completion of *Brahmacharya* (Student Life) or *Vaanaprastha* (Retired Life), to celebrate the renunciation of all worldly desires and absolute dedication to the service of mankind through spreading vedic wisdom.

Antyesti: Performed upon the death of the individual, when the body is consumed by fire and it's constituent elements are returned to Nature. This is the last ceremony and is also known as *Antyesti*, *Naramedha* and *Purusmedha*.

SOME VERY SPECIAL KOKANASTHA CUSTOMS

Bodan: While I have never attended a *bodan* and have never heard of anyone having one, this supposedly *Kokanastha* ritual is routinely performed by certain families after an auspicious function like a wedding, a *munja* (thread ceremony), a *barse* (naming ceremony) or even a *vaastu shanta* (a special *pooja* to propitiate the spirits of the soil that is being disturbed when constructing a house). Essentially, this special *pooja* is performed to ward off evil, to ensure the continuity of the family name and to make certain that the house enjoys peace and prosperity. According to the story of the *bodan*, the lady of the house who performs this *pooja* becomes the darling of her in-laws! There are two pre-conditions to doing a *bodan*: the house should not have a pregnant woman present, nor a cow that has just given birth. In this very female ceremony, no priest is required to officiate.

Barring the months of Chaitra and Paush, a *bodan* can be performed on any Tuesday or Friday in the year following the good occasion. Four married women and a young girl aged 5-8 (basically one who is pre-pubescent) representing the Mother Goddess are invited to do the *pooja* along with the lady of the house. Each woman is expected to bring one of the five ingredients that make up the *Panchamrut*– yoghurt, honey, ghee (*toop*), milk and sugar as her contribution to the *bodan*.

The ladies invited to participate in the *bodan* come early in the morning and first perform a *pooja* of the *tulsi* plant which is in the courtyard.

After a formal welcome, the ladies sit down to perform the *bodan* where they worship the Ganpati represented by a betel nut (*supari*) and his mother who is made out of wheat flour. The Mother Goddess is placed on a low stool (*paat*) and is given 5 garments, 5 lamps made out of sweetened boiled gram dal (*puran*) and 5 pieces of jewellery. The Goddess is worshipped by pouring yoghurt, honey, ghee (*toop*), milk and sugar over the idols. The lamps made of wheat and puran are mixed together and kneaded with a steady stream of ghee (*toop*) and milk offered by the five ladies and the young girl. This is known as the *bodan* and along with the *panchamrut* are offered as food for the gods (*neivedya*) and then distributed to everyone in the house as *prasad*. A reading of the story of the *bodan* precedes the lunch. Any remaining food is given to the family cow before the day is done.

The guests are given a lunch where the speciality is *puran poli*. The meal as always is followed by a gift (*dakshina*) and betel quid (*paan supari*).

This ritual which is normally performed by women with sons ensures that the family continues to prosper and flourish. However, like most of our traditions this too is slowly dying out and is performed very rarely, if at all. Some families, however, do it every year no matter what, and if they do happen to celebrate an occasion, the bodan is done the following year.

Laghurudra: Most *Kokanastha* families are worshippers of Shiva, a God who is especially honoured in the month of Shravan. The tradition of the *Laghurudra* has been carried forward in our family by Bapu *kaka*, my husband's youngest uncle who till very recently used to celebrate it in the family deity's temple at Dandeghar. This tiny hamlet just outside Panchgani has an old rock temple made in the Hemadpanthi-style of temple architecture. I can never forget one memorable *Laghurudra* when the entire clan had gathered to hear 11 Brahmin recite the *Rudra Stotra* eleven times each. While the walls of the temple resonated with 121 chants being recited, a steady trickle of water (abhishek) drizzling on the Shivling, a fresh water snake slithered up the water channel and seemed to bless us with his appearance.

The *Laghurudra* is actually a very simple *pooja* in keeping with Shiva's tough guy image. All that you really need is a wooden stool to lay out the *pooja*. You need to put a pair of betel nut leaves with a *supari* (betel nut) to represent the gods of the household, another set to represent Lord Ganesh, another one for Lord Shiva (Mahadev), yet another to represent the Brahmin, and the last set to represent oneself.

There is no need for floral decorations or special food since Shiva is supposed to be beyond all these trivialities. Nor is he fussy about the food offered to him so any simple food can be offered to him and distributed to those present as *prasad*. Once the custom of a *Laghurudra* is initiated, it is necessary to complete the cycle of eleven *Laghurudra*, after which the *Maharudra* is performed to indicate a closure. This very simple tradition can be performed by one person alone (if he can say the *Rudra Stotra* 121 times!) and does not even require eleven Brahmins for a *pooja* like this.

With our wedding ceremonies conducted in Sanskrit, most people find it hard to understand the *mantras* being recited around a fire, while relatives prattle around the bridal couple who are made to participate through a series of rituals. However, if one takes the trouble to find out what these actually mean, you will be amazed by their significance. Unlike most weddings which are noted for their noisy revelry, *Kokanastha* weddings are solemn, stark and simple. Infact, the *Kokanasthas* stand out in a mixed marriage celebration, their almost puritanical appearance of the *Kokanasthas* contrasting starkly with the other more exuberant party. However, all is not grim and gloomy and we do have our special *sarees*: the heavy silk handwoven *Paithani* in dazzling colours, woven gold designs (*buties*) and distinctive *padar*; the fine silk Narayanpeths in rich earthy colours with contrasting borders, or the mixed cotton and silk *Chanderi* and Indori *sarees*, their delicate gossamer beauty favoured by the older women. These gorgeous weaves offset with traditional jewellery mostly in gold or pearls are a must at any occasion.

Around fifteen days before the wedding, the mother of the groom/bride invites her friends along for a special Ganpati idol making ceremony. Each of the guests is asked to choose a handful of grain from five available to grind on the grinding stone (*jata*). This flour is made into a small ball of dough which represents Ganpati. This tiny home-made Ganpati is then stored in an air tight tin which is left either in the household pantry or near the family shrine. This invocation of Lord Ganesh is to ensure a smooth and happy wedding, after which, the Ganpati is made into multi-grain flour *kheer* which is distributed as *prasad*.

Traditionally, our weddings are 'arranged' through a person who brings the proposal to the boy's family on behalf of the girl's. Like everything else though, the concept of 'arranging' has changed and today couples are introduced to one another through friends or relatives or friends of friends. In today's internet age several couples even meet through matrimonial agencies or dating sites. How different from the days of my grandmother's time where she saw her husband only on her wedding day. Things were slightly different in my mother's time, but in conservative homes such as my mother-in-law's, her own mother only had a peek at her son-in law-to-be from behind the curtains, while the young man in question shyly looked at his bride to be, both not daring to look each other in the eye in the presence of their elders who actually discussed the wedding.

After the bride and groom approve of each other, the wedding date is fixed according to the stars, or the availability of the wedding hall. In the old days when families actually travelled to be present for the occasion, the wedding festivities were spread over several days. However, today the wedding ceremony is actually shorn of many of the pre-wedding customs. For instance, the *kelvan* insert, a party given by the relatives of the bride or the groom where the wedding gift is given, is almost a thing of the past with the entire family having a combined party. Similarly, the traditional bridal beauty treatment of the *haldi* ceremony where the bride's relatives smear her entire body with a paste of turmeric and sandalwood, and bathe her with milk has given way to the north Indian *sangeet* and *mehndi*.

Some pre-wedding ceremonies like the *Dev Devak* a small *pooja* where the house is blessed and God's grace sought for a hassle-free ceremony, the *Seemant poojan* where the groom and his family are welcomed to the village by the traditional washing of the feet and exchanging gifts, the *Vyahi Bhojan* – the dinner hosted by the groom's family are now very often ceremonies of the past.

Our weddings are usually held in the daytime, preferably before noon. On the morning of the ceremony the bride starts out with a pre-wedding *pooja* (*Gaurihaar*) where she prays before the idols of Annapoorna and Balkrishna given to her by her mother, for a happy and prosperous wedded life. She is dressed in a yellow *saree* traditionally given to her by her maternal uncle and which is worn throughout the first half of the wedding ceremony. After the girl is officially inducted into her new family, and puts on the *mangalsutra* she is given a new *saree* which she changes into, a deep, rich green to signify her entry into the realm of married women.

The bride is led into the *mandav* (the place where the wedding is solemnised), by her maternal uncle. One of the quaint customs of our weddings is the disappearance of the bride's mother while the *Mangalashtak* is being sung. The origin of this custom was basically to spare the mother the agony of watching her baby get married. The *Mangalashtak* which is a lyrical rendition describing the bride and the groom, their lives before they got married and how they now are starting out together, is normally a tuneless lament sung by a representative of each family but there are exceptions to this rule.

The groom on the other hand is brought into the *mandav* by five married women from the bride's family who welcome him with the traditional *aarti*. His feet are washed with water by the bride's mother and he is led to the wedding breakfast.

The groom's parents and family are seated at the table where they are given a traditional breakfast. Most times it is a toss up between *pohe, saboodanyachi khichadi* and *upama* with some *laadoo* or *shira* thrown in.

The basic Vedic ceremony consists of several rituals:

Gaurihaar: A special *pooja* performed only by the bride prior to the actual wedding ceremony. She prays to the special deities of Baby Krishna and Annapoorna that she takes along with her to her new home asking them for their blessings.

Antarpaat: The groom and bride stand on either side of a cloth held between them. At the appointed auspicious time, the cloth between them is dropped and they garland each other.

Kanyadaan: The father offers his daughter's hand to her groom and asks him to look after her.

Mangalsutra bandhan: The groom ties the "holy thread" around the neck of his new bride promising to look after her.

Saptapadi: Life's journey represented by the seven mounds of rice which the husband and wife go through.

Lajja hom: The last ritual where both the husband and wife propitiate the fire with popped wheat (lhaya).

The wedding ceremonies are conducted under a canopy decorated with flowers or swags with siblings of the bridal couple standing behind them. The *karavali* (maid of honour) one each, for both the groom and the bride carries a lighted lamp and the brother of the bride has to be on hand to twist the ear of the groom, warning him subtly that should he not look after his sister properly, there will be more to come.

The religious ceremonies over, the groom points out the North Star (*Dhruv tara*) to his new bride assuring her that his love for her would be constant as the star. But since most of our weddings are conducted in broad daylight, spotting the star is impossible!

We also have another game where a ring immersed in a bucket has to be fished out by the bride and groom, the rationale being that he who gets it first wears the pants in the family. In yet another custom, the girl eats a *paan* that is offered to her after the lunch and if her tongue becomes a deep red, it signifies her husband's undying and deep love. But of all the fun and games associated with the wedding festivities, the most looked forward to game is the 'Feeding of the spouse with a witty ditty'. Since it was considered inauspicious and rude to address one's husband by his name, a wedding or a *munja* is the only time a woman was allowed to publicly address him by his name. The bride is expected to feed her groom after using his name in a witty rhyme. Naturally, this makes a bride blush and giggle and her gaffes and goof ups are a great source of amusement to the assembled guests who are only waiting to pounce on that mix-up or confusion.

After the wedding ceremony, all the guests are invited to participate in the wedding feast. Traditionally this is a sit-down meal served on banana leaves, and consists of two three kinds of rice (Bhaat (page 35), Masaale Bhaat (page 40) and Dahi Bhaat (page 46)), one usal, one bhaaji, one *koshimbir, panchamrut*, pickles, *papad* and crisps, and the essential five sweets (*panchapakwaan*). Special care is given to ensure that the groom's favourite sweets are catered for, and usually, *shrikhand, baasundi, kheer, sheera, puran poli, jalebi, karanji* and even *laadoo* will be on the menu. However, at today's weddings, the *panchapakwan* meal is given short shrift, and sweets are restricted to two or three at most. It is strange but the hot *jalebis* that are served as a specialty at weddings today, were once considered the cheapest sweet on the menu, and a 'jalebi wedding' was signified a skinflint of a father of the bride.

Grihapravesh: After all the ceremonies are over, the bride is escorted to her new home by her brother, where she is welcomed by her new family. As she steps into the house, she gently kicks a pot of rice ensuring that she brings good luck with her.

Aluche Khatkhate

GRAVIED COLOCASIA LEAVES WITH PEANUTS

No wedding feast can be a success without this typical patal *bhaaji*.

Ingredients

4-5 colocasia leaves (arviche *paan* or *alu*)

½ cup soaked peanuts

½ cup split Bengal gram (*chana dal*), soaked

2 tablespoons gram flour

Jaggery to taste

Seasoning

1 teaspoon oil

¼ teaspoon mustard seeds

¼ teaspoon turmeric powder

Method

- Cook the leaves and the split Bengal gram till soft. Mash well with a vegetable masher.
- For the seasoning, heat the oil and add the mustard seeds. When they start to splutter, add turmeric powder.
- Add peanuts and mashed *dal* and colocasia leaves mixture and continue cooking.

- In a bowl, mix together the gram flour and enough water to make a thick paste. Add to the colocasia mixture and continue to cook. Watch it boil and bubble (*khat khat*).
- When almost done, stir in some jaggery.

Note: This recipe is not intended to serve guests for a wedding feast, but should suffice for a regular meal for 4 people.

Other dishes served at a wedding feast include Masaale Bhaat (page 40), Bharli Vaangi (page 80), Birdyachi Usal (page 93), Flower ani Batatyacha Rassa (page 63), *papad,* Kurdaya (page 127, 128), Puri (page 132).

SATYANARAYAN POOJA

This special prayer of thanksgiving is usually performed after an important or auspicious function or event, and can be performed by the newly married couple, a successful student, even a single woman. Actually, anyone who has a reason to thank God for his blessings. Apart from performing the *pooja*, one has to feed the gods and a married couple (*mehun*). Like a *haldi-kunku*, one never refuses an invitation to a Satyanarayan *pooja*. The rich sweetness of the *Prasad*, usually *sheera*, makes it worth one's while.

Sheera

SWEET SEMOLINA WITH BANANAS

Ingredients

1 ¼ cups ghee (*toop*)
1 ¼ cups semolina
1 ¼ cups milk
1 ¼ cups sugar
1 ¼ bananas, sliced or mashed
3-4 saffron threads
1 teaspoon cardamom powder
5-6 almonds, soaked, peeled and slivered

Method

- Heat the ghee in a *kadai* and add the semolina. Stir continuously till the semolina turns light brown and fragrant.
- Lower the heat and add milk, stirring continuously to ensure no lumps are formed. Cook, covered, till done.
- Add the sugar and bananas and continue cooking, covered, till the sugar melts.
- Stir in saffron, cardamom powder and slivered almonds.

Note: Especially for the *pooja*, the *prasad* must be made with 1 and ¼ measures of semolina, sugar, ghee (*toop*) and milk. Depending on the amount of *sheera* to be made, the measure could be 1¼ cups, *vati* or bowl. Today we reduce the quantity of ghee (*toop*), as the *sheera* can become far too heavy, but this should not be done for the *Satyanarayan Prasad*. On top of the *sheera* ¼ of a banana, which is sliced, is added to make up the banana component which is essential for the *prasad*. One can also add powdered cardamom, saffron and almond slivers for added richness and flavour. It can also be made as regular snack without the banana.

Ghavlechi Kheer

WHEAT PASTA PUDDING

This is my favourite *kheer* made out of sun-dried pasta fashioned out of wholewheat flour. Perhaps it is the process of rolling out minute quantities of stiffly kneaded wheat flour between the forefinger and thumb to get tiny wheat grain-sized pasta, which are left to dry out in the sun, which gives this pudding a unique flavour.

Ingredients

1 teaspoon ghee (*toop*)
1 cup *ghavle* (wholewheat pasta)
2 cups hot milk
½ cup sugar
3-4 saffron threads
½ teaspoon cardamom powder

Method

- Heat the ghee on a *tawa* and lightly roast the *ghavle* till fragrant.
- Transfer the *ghavle* to a pan and add hot milk and bring the mixture to the boil. Depending on how thick you want it, adjust the quantity of milk.
- Add sugar to taste, saffron threads and cardamom powder.
- Serve hot or cold.

Note: The menu at all special occasions must contain *kheer*. The *kheer* should either be made out of *ghavle* (wholewheat pasta) or *sevaiya* (vermicelli). Rice *kheer* is not normally served on auspicious days.

Batatyachi Bhaaji

SPICY POTATOES

This particular way of cooking potatoes is not only very easy, but also a guaranteed crowd-pleaser.

Ingredients

3-4 medium potatoes, boiled, peeled and chopped into large pieces

Salt to taste

A pinch of sugar

Grated coconut, for garnishing

Chopped coriander, for garnishing

Seasoning

1-2 tablespoons oil

½ teaspoon mustard seeds

¼ teaspoon turmeric powder

¼ teaspoon asafoetida (*hing*)

2-3 curry leaves

1 green chilli, chopped (optional)

Method

- For the seasoning, heat the oil in a *kadai* and add the mustard seeds. When they start to splutter, add turmeric powder, asafoetida, curry leaves and salt. Add the green chilli and stir.
- Add the chopped potato and mix well.
- Add a pinch of sugar, stir and garnish with grated coconut and coriander.

Two kinds of rice are a must –Varan Bhaat (page 34, 35) and Masaale Bhaat (page 40). Taak (page 212) is also mandatory as is the Panchamrut (page 12). In addition to the guests of honour (*mehun* or married couple), one must also feed the priest. Also remember, that the first plate of food is offered to the gods and is served without salt.

Suralichya Vadya

SAVOURY GRAM FLOUR ROLLS

This is one of the staples of my kitchen and is almost *de rigeur* at my special meals. This is my way of using up the *taak* that remains after the butter is separated from the milk when I make *loni* (white butter) for the ghee (*toop*). So, in a fashion, this is the ultimate recipe for using up left-overs. And the *suralichya vadya*, I can guarantee, will never be left over. Not even the crumbs!

Ingredients

1 cup gram flour (*besan*)
3 cups *taak* (see note)
½ teaspoon turmeric powder
½ teaspoon salt
A pinch of asafoetida (*hing*)
2 tablespoons chopped coriander
2 tablespoons grated coconut

Seasoning

1 tablespoon oil
½ teaspoon mustard seeds

Method

- Place the gram flour in a bowl and add the taak, turmeric powder, salt and asafoetida and whisk well to ensure that there are no lumps.
- Transfer the mixture to a *kadai* on high heat, stirring continuously. It is essential to have a large *kadai* or pan because as the mixture boils vigorously, it will splatter all over the stove if given a chance!
- To check if the mixture is ready, dip the whisk into the mixture, when the whisk is lifted, the mixture should cling to the wire and leave a trail behind. At that stage the mixture appears glossy.
- Lower the heat and pour the mixture into a *taat* (a flat stainless steel plate with a rim) while still hot and spread the mixture evenly to get a 2 mm thick layer. Set aside to dry for 10-15 minutes. You will need a total of 3 *taat* for this quantity of mixture.
- For the seasoning, heat the oil in a *kadai* and fry the mustard seeds until they start to splutter. Pour the seasoning over the set mixture in the *taat*.
- Sprinkle finely chopped coriander and grated coconut and roll it up like a Swiss roll. Cut into bite-sized pieces. Place in the refrigerator and serve cold.

Note: Make *taak* by adding 3 cups water to 1 cup yoghurt. This recipe is easy, but requires some practice. You have to be careful that the set mixture is neither over nor under cooked. Also, the layer should not be too thin nor too thick or it will be difficult to roll up.

Vaangyache Kaap

BRINJAL FRITTERS

Ingredients

1 large (250 grams) brinjal
½ teaspoon salt
¼ teaspoon turmeric powder
½ teaspoon red chilli powder
2 tablespoons gram flour
1 cup oil for deep-frying

Method

- Wash and pat the brinjal dry. Cut into thick ½-inch slices.
- Mix together the salt, turmeric and chilli powders and rub evenly over the sliced brinjal.
- Dip the slice in gram flour till well coated on both sides.
- Deep-fry the brinjals until brown on both sides.

MOTHER AND BABY FOOD

Traditionally, the first trimester of a pregnancy is kept a secret mainly because there are chances of things going wrong, but once the three months have been crossed it is difficult to keep things under wraps! There are lots of foods which are to be avoided during pregnancy and many of the common no-no's are foods which are considered 'heaty' like papayas and mangoes. The new mother-to-be is encouraged to think positive thoughts and especially a first time mum is pampered and spoilt no end.

AFTER THE BABY IS BORN

The first baby is normally delivered in the mother's maternal home as she would be more comfortable there, so traditionally the girl goes home to her maternal home in her seventh month (after which it is supposed to be dangerous to travel) and stays till the baby is forty days old. The new mother and child are expected to stay in a darkened room for forty days in semi-isolation. Of course visitors are allowed but general activity is restricted .The mother and baby are treated to a daily massage and oil bath with the mother's stomach corseted in a tightly bound *saree*. The new mother is encouraged to eat foods that make her back strong and give her back energy and vitality. The first visit outside the home for a new mother and her baby is a visit to Sitaladevi Temple, or temple of the Goddess of smallpox. However, many of these traditions are not followed today.

Dinkache Laadoo

RICH DRIED FRUIT RESIN BALLS

These delicious *laadoo* are hardly ever made at home, and are eaten by everyone else but the mother they are meant for. Edible gum or gaund in Hindi and the smooth, black *bibba* (*bilawar*) seeds of the marking nut tree (*Semecarpus anacardium*) are known to have restorative properties which are ideal for a mother recuperating after delivery.

Ingredients

1 kg edible gum/resin crystals (*dink*)
1 kg ghee (*toop*)
½ kg grated dried coconut
½ kg seedless dried dates (*kharik*)
½ kg poppy seeds (*khus khus*)
½ kg almonds
100 grams *bibba* seeds
¾ kg sugar or grated jaggery

Method

- Place in a large *kadai* the gum crystals and ghee and roast on low heat till the crystals pop. Set aside to cool and then grind to a fine powder.
- In the same *kadai* roast the grated coconut, dried dates, poppy seeds, almonds and *bibba* seeds. Set aside to cool and then grind to a coarse powder.
- Mix together both the powders and heat in a pan for 2 minutes on low heat. Take off the heat and add grated jaggery and mix well.
- To make the *laadoo*, grease your palms with a little ghee and shape into *laadoo* while the mixture is still warm.

Alivache Laadoo

SWEET COCONUT AND GARDEN CRESS BALLS

I personally have never liked these *laadoo*, but many find them irresistible.

Ingredients

1 cup garden cress seeds (*aliv*)
Coconut water from 2 coconuts
4 cups grated coconut
½ kg jaggery

Method

- Soak the seeds in coconut water for 2 hours.
- Add the grated coconut and jaggery and cook till all the water dries up. Make sure that you stir from time to time to prevent it from scorching.
- Cool and shape into *laadoo*.

Note: These *laadoo* can also be eaten during a fast (*upavas*).

ALL GOOD THINGS MUST COME TO AN END

Unfortunately this is true for all of us. Like birth, death is one of the 16 *sanskar* we have to go through. On the thirteenth day of the bereavement, the family has the terava or the *pooja* where all the invitees offer their respects to the deceased. This ceremony marks the end of the mourning period and is normally followed by a lunch.

The menu for this is also prescribed. As mentioned earlier, no salt should be served in the *taat*. The chutney which is normally served is made out of *kokum* and the *koshimbir* is usually a Bhoplyache Bhareet (page 108). Other essentials on this menu are a rice Kheer (page 217), Wade (page 216) and Karlyachi Bhaaji (page 217). As with all other occasions, Varan Bhaat (page 34, 35) is a must. Usually, the special sweet for the day will be a favourite of the deceased. Since this is a day of mourning, the food is generally white in colour, hence the *laadoo* that are distributed after the feast as *prasad* are normally Ravyache Laadoo (page 188).

Amsulachi Chutney

KOKUM CHUTNEY

This sour chutney is served on this the thirteenth day of bereavement.

Ingredients

½ cup dried *kokum* rinds
2-3 cardamoms
Salt to taste
Sugar to taste

Method

- Soak the dried *kokum* for 2 hours prior to making the chutney.
- Grind to a fine paste with cardamom seeds and salt. Add sugar to adjust the sourness.

Wade

DEEP-FRIED BLACK GRAM PUFFED BREADS

These wade are *puri* made from *udid dal* flour.

Ingredients

2 cups skinless split black gram flour (*urad dal* flour, made from washed and dried dal, coarsely ground to the consistency of fine *rava*)
Salt to taste
1 tablespoon oil + for deep-frying

Method

- Knead the flour with water, salt, and 1 tablespoon oil and set aside to rest for at least 1 hour.
- Heat the oil in a *kadai* and roll out the dough into small puri.
- Deep-fry and serve.

Karlyachi Bhaaji

SPICED BITTER GOURD

Ingredients

½ kg bitter gourd, thinly sliced
Salt to taste
½ teaspoon red chilli powder
Sugar to taste
Lime juice to taste
1 cup grated dried coconut
1 tablespoon coriander leaves

Seasoning

1 tablespoon oil
¼ teaspoon mustard seeds
¼ teaspoon asafoetida (*hing*)
¼ teaspoon turmeric powder

Method

- Reduce bitterness from the gourd by sprinkling some salt over the slices. Wrap them in a napkin, place a weight on top for about 30 minutes.
- For the seasoning, heat oil in a *kadai*; add mustard seeds and when they begin to splutter, add asafoetida, turmeric powder and bitter gourd and stir-fry till crisp.
- Add chilli powder, salt, sugar and lime juice to taste and mix well. Add grated coconut, mix and garnish with chopped coriander.

Kheer

RICE PUDDING

Ingredients

1 litre milk
1 cup cooked rice
½ cup sugar
2-3 saffron threads
½ teaspoon cardamom powder

Method

- Bring the milk to a boil. Add the rice and simmer till the milk thickens. Add the sugar, the saffron and cardamom powder.
- Cook till it thickens slightly. Serve cold.

Glossary

English	Hindi	Marathi
Amaranth	Chouli/Chavli	Laal/hirvi maath
Banana flower	Kele ka phool	Kelfool
Beaten rice	Poha	Pohe
Bengal gram, roasted split	Daalia	
Bengal gram, split	Chana dal	Chanya chi dal
Bitter gourd	Karela	Karle
Black gram, skinless split	Dhuli urad dal	Udid dal
Black gram, split	Chilkewali urad dal	Udid dal
Black gram, whole	Sabut urad	Udid
Bottle gourd	Lauki	Doodhi
Cardamoms, green	Elaichi	Veldode
Carom leaves	Ajwain ke patte	Owyachi pana
Colostrum	Khiis	Poss
Dill	Suva bhaji	Shepu
Dried coconut	Khopra	Khobre
Dried white peas	Sookhe safed matar	Suke Watane
Drumsticks	Saijan ki Phalli	Shevgyacha shenga
Fenugreek seeds	Methi dana	Methi
Field beans	Semi	Dalimbya
Gram flour	Besan	Chanyacha pith
Green gram, skinless split	Dhuli moong dal	Mooga chi cal
Green gram, sprouted	Ankurit moong	Mode alele moong
Jackfruit	Kathal	Phanas
Madras cucumber		Kakdi
Malabar spinach	Vali bhaji	Mayalu
Musk melon	Kharbooj	Chibad
Parboiled rice	Ukda chawal	Ukade tandool
Pigeon peas, split	Toovar dal/Arhar dal	Turi chi dal
Red pumpkin	Kaddu	Bhopla
Refined flour	Maida	Maida
Rice flour	Chawal ka atta	Tandla chi pithi
Ridge gourd	Turai	Ghosale
Semolina	Rawa/Sooji	Rava
Yam	Zamikand/suran	Suran